THE KNOWLEDGE REVOLUTION

THE KNOWLEDGE
REVOLUTION

An Analysis of the International Brain Market

by
D. N. CHORAFAS

McGRAW-HILL BOOK COMPANY

NEW YORK ST. LOUIS SAN FRANCISCO

Library of Congress Catalog Card Number: 78-110250
Published and distributed in the United States
by McGraw-Hill Book Company, 1970

10808

TO GUSTAVE O. ARLT

FOREWORD

BY GUSTAVE O. ARLT

The term 'Brain Drain' is a fairly recent coinage but the process which it describes is as old as Western civilization itself. Its causes, over the centuries, have been various; its effects upon the countries that were its beneficiaries were highly salubrious; its effects on the victimized countries were usually disastrous. Some brain drain eras were protracted but calm and peaceful; some were brief, stormy and spectacular.

The first recorded brain drain in Western civilization took place during the reign of Ptolemy Soter in Alexandria when great numbers of intellectuals emigrated from Athens to the attractive atmosphere of the Ptolemaic court with its incredible library. The conditions in both the losing and receiving state were characteristic: Athens had outlived its Golden Age and was falling into decay; Alexandria had a burgeoning culture and actively recruited Athenian intellectuals. Athens never recovered from its brain drain.

One of the most spectacular episodes in intellectual history resulted from the fall of the Byzantine Empire and the capture and sacking of Constantinople, first by the army of the Fourth Crusade (1204), then by Sultan Mohammed II (1453). The artistic, literary and scientific wealth of the city-state before the disaster was almost inconceivable. The mass migration of intellectuals from Constantinople to Europe was directly responsible for the cultural revival of Europe, for the end of the Dark Ages, for Humanism and the Renaissance. The emigrants established the great centres of learning, first at Padua, followed by Oxford, Prague, Heidelberg and many others. Without the brain drain from Constantinople, it is hard to imagine what the later history of Europe might have been. It need hardly be added that Constantinople, though soon rebuilt by the Turks, never recovered its cultural and scientific leadership.

America profited by several minor but significant brain drains in the nineteenth century. The first of these began when Robert Owen,

7

a Scots industrialist with socialistic ideas, arrived with his 'Ship-
load of Knowledge', to establish in 1825 the town of New Harmony
and the beginnings of manufacturing industry on the lower Ohio
River. Much more important in numbers and significance was the
emigration of several thousand German intellectuals after the ill-
fated democratic revolution in Prussia in 1848. One of the chief
beneficiaries of that movement was the American elementary and
secondary public school system. Many schools to this day still
carry the name of Carl Schurz, one of the leading figures in the
emigration of 1848.

In more recent times the greatest mass exodus of scientists,
scholars, writers and artists from Europe mostly to America was
set off by the rise of Adolf Hitler and National Socialism. It began
as a trickle in 1930, grew to a stream by 1934 and rose to a flood
after 1938. Its effects on Europe as well as America are incalculable.
The very outcome of the Second World War was to a great extent
determined by this brain drain. Germany's failure to develop atomic
weapons resulted largely from the loss of the best scientific brains.
America's efforts on the other hand, were vastly strengthened by
the brilliant *émigrés*, to mention only Albert Einstein and Enrico
Fermi.

Now, in the 1960s, we are in a period of brain drain of world-wide
proportions, painstakingly described with great perception and deli-
cate sensitivity in this book by Dr D. N. Chorafas. The remedies he
suggests are reasonable and should have been obvious to the governments and industrial establishments of Europe, particularly of
England, long ago. Unhappily, the ossification of these structures
is so advanced as to make it highly unlikely that adequate measures
will be taken before it is too late. America will continue to need
more highly trained brains than she can produce and she will continue to import them.

It is not difficult to predict that by the early 1970s the brain
drain will grow far beyond its present state. Between 1956 and
1966, the annual production of Ph.D.s in U.S. universities rose
from 8,903 to 17,500. In 1967, 18,000 Ph.D.s were awarded and

this year there will be 21,600. Large as these numbers are, the demand is even larger. But now the Selective Service Act of 1967 forbids the deferment from military service of students entering graduate school after September of that year. The result of this insane piece of legislation will be that in 1968 and 1969 roughly forty per cent of all young men called to military service will be graduate students or recent college graduates. The full impact will strike three years later when the entering classes of 1968 should begin to receive their doctoral degrees. Instead of the projected 24,900 new Ph.D.s in 1971, there will be only 14,940. In 1972, instead of 26,800 there will be only 15,080. And in 1973 the projected number will drop from 32,000 to 19,200. In other words, the production of Ph.D.s in the United States will be set back a full five years.

Obviously the demand for highly trained brain power for business, industry, education and government will continue to rise. Just as obviously America will not produce it in sufficient numbers. Where then to look for it? The answer is as obvious as the premises.

GUSTAVE O. ARLT,

A.B., M.A., PH.D., LL.B., LITT.D.

*President, Council of Graduate Schools
in the United States of America*

Washington, D.C.
July, 1968

CONTENTS

INTRODUCTION

This book has been written to discuss Europe's economic and cultural future against the whole background of the world market for brains. It examines the role of industry, governments and universities in meeting the challenge of the 1970s and thereafter.

The realization that a modern economy's most important capital resource is not money, raw materials or equipment but *brains* has been slow in coming. This fact is the kernel of the Knowledge Revolution.

The long-term economic and social prosperity of a country depends on the knowledge available to it. Progress is based on knowledge—and knowledge is used by brains and increased by brains. Books are often thought to be the most significant embodiments of knowledge, but they are merely passive repositories. Human brain power is the key to the future.

The notion that human brains and talent are a most vital form of industrial capital may seem self-evident and trivial but it is nevertheless true that the awareness that progress can be seriously impeded by *lack* of talent has only developed acutely during the last eight years, following the tremendous international attention paid to the so-called 'Brain Drain'. People now realize that a flow of brains—of talented, trained, experienced people—away from a country is at least as serious in the long run as a flow of money. The tardiness of this realization has largely been due to the determination over the last hundred years to regard men in general as a source of labour rather than of wisdom. But modern industry is based on man's science, not on his physical effort, and science depends on (indeed, *is*) knowledge.

It is argued in this book that the brain drain from Europe is merely a symptom of a basic disease in the European economic system. The brain drain is one of the most manifest symptoms of the European sickness, which is why it is analysed in some detail early in this book.

Recent US Immigration legislation—which is discussed later—may well reduce the extent of the brain drain, but will have no effect (except perhaps a harmful one) on the basic reasons why brains *want* to leave Europe.

The men leaving England and the rest of Europe today are no longer mainly peasants and factory workers. They are scientists, technologists, doctors, planners, and professional men who are still proudly British, French, German, or Italian, but who have abandoned hope of proper recognition and progress in their country of origin. This is the essence of the brain drain. Migration is the reaction of disappointed men.

The brain drain is a symptom, not a cause of decay. The causes are more generic and deep-rooted. As the loss of able men and women brings about a further dilution of a European economic structure that is already weak, it brings into perspective some of the reasons for its decay. If nothing is done, a situation could arise where Europe will earn a living from its technological industries but the United States will own them. This is not what Europe wants or needs.

The answer lies in imaginative planning, but Europe's leaders continue along the same tried paths. Instead of expanding opportunity, they have reduced it; instead of dispensing with senile leadership and rusty organization, they have built around themselves branches of minor theology; instead of pulling down old structures, they have put battlements on them; instead of enjoying the present and working for the future, they continue to plead for the impossible return of yesterday.

The future has always been the province of those who have planned for it. Europe is not planning for its future at this moment in any significant way. Its research endeavours are still chaotic in scope and vision. Its universities are not progressive, and the uncertain industrial and governmental policies of European nations have been overtaken by evolution.

It is time for the leading European nations to stop deceiving themselves. The success of America's massive recruiting campaigns

in persuading European or Asian engineers and scientists to emigrate is only possible because of the conditions prevailing within
these continents. Compulsory barriers would aggravate the situation. Only brighter opportunities in the country of origin can stop
the flow of brains away from it.

London's *Financial Times* has proposed that American investment should be controlled in the way that France has already
attempted. That restricting American companies might evoke industrial retaliation is evident. Less evident, and far more worrying,
is that such short-sightedness could bring Europe's standard of
living into a state of stagnation. Protectionist moves no longer succeed today as they did in the past; not only does Europe have an
excess of protectionism, but protectionism (in lieu of incentives)
has become a chief cause of decay. Control over the emigration of
brains is similarly impractical.

Mr Anthony Wedgwood Benn, speaking in the House of Com-
mons in a debate on the brain drain in February 1967, commented:

'Any sort of control [on emigration] would be impractical to
enforce, unjust to apply and would infringe personal liberty. It
would stimulate the desire to escape among others who might never
otherwise think of leaving.'

Our research in forty-three countries of Europe, Asia, Africa and
South America indicates that few have yet recognized the value of
ability. As a result, the brains elude them and go to America. For
a future holding the most formidable challenges and the greatest
rewards in history we must strive to create the conditions in Europe
under which our most able men will choose to do their best work.

Part I

THE IMPACT OF THE BRAIN DRAIN

Chapter One

THE BRAIN DRAIN
AND THE BRAIN MARKET

Unto every one that hath shall be given, and he
shall have abundance : but from him that hath
not shall be taken away even that which he hath.
                                St Matthew xxv. 29

During the last few years, discovery of the extent of the brain drain
has stunned governments and industrial leaders, and presented
them with a complex of questions for which nothing in their past
experience has prepared the answers. How much do we care about
the migration of our scientists? At what point does this migration
become a drain? How is the drain going to affect industry and the
economy? Does the brain drain, in the long term, constitute a
service or a disservice to humanity at large? Is the brain drain
only symptomatic of a much larger problem?

In our introduction we said that the brain drain was a symptom,
not a cause, of industrial decay. So before discussing the drain itself
let us look at the central problem. It can be defined very simply.
We are entering an era in which only the mass-oriented industries
will be able to compete in world markets. This state of affairs can
only harden in the Knowledge Revolution—and the Technological
Age it defines. And the Knowledge Revolution promises to be as
great an upheaval in its way as the Industrial Revolution was in
its time.

Mass manufacture and mass marketing demand long-term planning of a complexity which only governments can provide, for it
will involve social upheaval, a new university system, political integration with other countries, and other matters beyond the scope

of industry alone. But do governments have the courage to lead into social change of this magnitude? History shows that they do not.

The most important precondition of mass industry is R & D. Research and Development, too, can be undertaken on a mass scale. It is because only America and Russia have so far recognized this fact that most R & D work today is being carried out within their borders. Table I shows that R & D expenditure within the US is massive, and constantly rising.

TABLE I

United States Expenditure of Research and Development Funds in Various Sectors, 1959-68

$ million

	Total	Federal Government	Industry	Universities and colleges	Associated Federal contract research centres	Other non-profit institutions
1959	12,520	1640	9620	680	340	240
1960	13,710	1730	10,510	830	360	280
1961	14,500	1870	10,910	970	410	340
1962	15,610	2100	11,460	1140	470	440
1963	17,350	2280	12,630	1360	530	550
1964	19,180	2840	13,510	1590	630	610
1965 (preliminary)	20,470	3090	14,200	1870	640	670
1966 (estimated)	22,220	3260	15,400	2180	650	730
1967 (estimated)	23,800	3360	16,610	2360	680	790
1968 (estimated)	25,000	3500	17,300	2600	700	900

Source: U.S. National Science Foundation

This sort of programme demands a huge labour force of highly talented scientists and technologists, so massive that even America cannot produce it alone. But she is not worrying: while the need for brains exists, the brains will gather in the United States, for the financial rewards, for the research opportunity, for professional horizons, for creative conditions.

That is it in a nutshell, and the remainder of our book will investigate this problem more closely and attempt to offer some solutions to Europe's dilemma. This major problem once solved, or even tackled intelligently, and the brain drain will be plugged—not mechanically but organically. The flow will be turned off at source, only if and when the source of the ill is tackled. Questions of protectionist immigration legislation would become irrelevant if the reasons for migration were properly studied and tackled.

But first let us look at what we are losing. It is often considered that the brain drain only concerns men trained in science and technology. This, though correct as it stands, is not broad enough. In our judgment there should be added two more classes of people. The first includes all other university graduates, whether in literature, art, medicine, law, or any profession requiring university training. The other includes the self-made men who go up the social and organizational ladder to reach positions of leadership and command in industry and government.

The drain of scientists is not our only concern; the loss of intellect and 'guts' in any field of industry, scientific or not, is also a serious dissipation of a country's economic strength. It is likely that emigrants, as such, are more than averagely ambitious, mentally and physically fit, possessing a fair degree of courage and initiative. They are in every way the young men Europe can least afford to lose. One way in which their migration could have a permanent effect on a nation's future has been pointed out by Dr John Gibson, a Cambridge geneticist:

'The problem has socio-biological significance, for the migrants may contribute to the gene pool of the population to which they have moved, or, having returned after marrying and/or reproducing abroad, make a different contribution to the gene pool of their parent population to that which they would otherwise have made.'

Any comment on the loss of talented men should ideally be based on qualitative as well as on quantitative estimates. The cerebral wealth of a nation is not made up of cold statistics but of millions of individual personalities. Statistics can be useful (when accurate) but tend to present too many facts with too little insight.

Emigration involves many difficult personal decisions. Women are, on the whole, social creatures, and while a man may be quite prepared to start life afresh in another continent, his wife may be far more reluctant to leave the social circle she is in. A man has also to consider the lives of his children; particularly the educational system in which they will grow to maturity and the professional environment within which they will struggle for life. There is thus a vast complex of aspects that anyone considering emigration has to try to evaluate. The decision to migrate is not a simple matter.

The heart of the issue lies in the availability of professional opportunity. It is conceivable that if many graduates do not emigrate in future years, they will find themselves among the ranks of the unemployed unless they change their profession or status. It would seem hardly fair that a nation should educate a man to expect a certain way of life and then deny it to him. British industry says it wants more graduates, but is it ready to use them? If the brain drain completely halted tomorrow, would there be even 'low-paid'[1] work for the scientists and technologists to do? One British Ph.D. said to me:

'I do not give England more than five years of scientific and technological survival. I wish to stay and work in England. I am afraid the way things are going in my country I will have to migrate to the United States within a few years.

'Even young students today look for the proper background to sell their services in the US. If this situation continues for long, there will be an uprising.'[2]

This statement may sound an alarmist one but it comes from a

---

[1] But why low-paid and not highly paid creative work, after all?

[2] In May 1968, during a Parliamentary debate, Technology Minister Anthony Wedgwood Benn said roughly the same about his concern that the student fever in France might spread to Britain.

reliable source. They are the words of a senior lecturer in the science department of a north of England university. His reference was visionary. The explosion of the young generation he was fore-telling happened across the Channel a few months later. One could read on the walls during the May 1968 Sorbonne uprising: *'L'Imagination au pouvoir!'* This is what European youth is yearn-ing for and no government during the last quarter of a century has been able to find a means of answering this profound and legitimate claim in a satisfactory manner.

The reasons why people contemplate migration are rooted in every aspect of the opportunities offered by the environment. The threat of possible unemployment, the periodic freezes on salary increases, and the present gloomy prospects for capital investment are making many able people doubtful about the future for their skills. Not surprisingly, much of the interest in working abroad seems to be an emotional reaction to the current conditions of stag-nation. This is a vicious cycle. The march to industrial and techno-logical progress today should be led by the very men who emigrate in the brain drain.

As a senior Scandinavian banker commented: 'Many of our men leave for greener fields. What makes a field greener is not the colour of the dollar but the opportunity a man expects to find there, and the pleasanter working environment.' Even professional opportunity-watchers admit that the possibilities for professional development at home have not kept pace with the aspirations of the younger generation. Fleming Kolby, a Dane by origin, who emigrated to California, became Vice President of the Bank of America, then returned to Copenhagen as the director for Scan-dinavia of the world's largest bank, has said:

'The freedom to develop is a tremendous force. The American competitive system is hard on those who are unwilling or unable, but it is also highly rewarding to those who are able and willing men. Professional development and risk go hand in hand. Freedom to develop also means freedom to get trapped, freedom to fail. That is how better, more competitive people are seasoned.

'In Europe, by contrast, development goes step by step. Extreme examples left aside, the European executive or scientist moves too slowly for his own good or for the good of his country. Class distinction still weighs too heavily. This turns the personal drive sour and accounts for a good deal of the unwillingness to accept responsibility. The whole system should change, and change must start with the right kind of education.'

This is no news to sane members of our society, but somehow its meaning gets lost in the stalemate of present-day conditions. As *The Economist* has aptly stated:

'Scientists leave home for two reasons and money is only one of them. An able research man gravitates, like a pin to a magnet, to the place where work that most interests him is being done, and at the moment, because of its huge science budget, much of that work is being done in the United States. And so they emigrate there. Lord Shackleton admitted during the House of Lords debate on the brain drain (How many leave? No one knows) that "the movement of professionally qualified people . . . has reached such proportions that it now constitutes a major international problem".'

In March 1967 Dr Leon Goldberg left his job as director of the British Industrial Biological Research Association to join the Albany Medical College, New York, at a lower salary. The reasons that made him decide to emigrate centred around the difficulty of finding suitable staff. An equally critical reason was insufficient industrial support for the research association's work on the effect of chemicals on food and drink. Said Dr Goldberg: 'I suppose we shall be emigrating for good, but it is certainly not for money . . . [the new assignment] will be like taking a leap ten years ahead compared with here.'

Another cause of Europe's brain drain is the foolishness of its 'stop-go' policies. The results will be disastrous if our best talent feels that the proposals to get European technology moving are tentative, shaky and unsound. Such men will be watching with caution and curiosity to see what sort of policies the European governments will evolve, and they will be suspicious of any inconsistent or faltering steps. Governments must go out of their way to prove their sincerity and determination not to waste their scientific talent.

Scandinavia is an example of a closed brain drain circuit—and since Sweden is one of the few European countries for which reliable statistics are available, we can take Scandinavia as a case study on brain drain and brain gain. Inasmuch as countries have immigration as well as emigration of talent the brain drain is to some extent offset by a 'brain gain'. But any 'gain' must be examined closely from the qualitative point of view, since a country tends to gain from the less developed countries and lose to the advanced ones.

As Professor Engström commented during our discussion on the 'balance of payments' in ability:

'Sweden has definitely lost to America some top scientists who did not find here a fertile soil for work in their fields. This includes doctors, mathematicians and engineers. Sweden has gained men from the other Scandinavian countries, and has also attracted able men from the continent of Europe. Numerically, this give a slightly positive balance, but qualitatively the balance is not equal.'

Dr Göran Friborg has calculated the net balance of scientists, technologists, economists and doctors after gain and drain, and his findings are given in Table II.

Scandinavian universities turn out large numbers of young intellectuals, and the Scandinavian countries have a healthy industry, especially in the field of advanced technology. Denmark alone exports half the electronic equipment it produces. But the area suffers a brain drain of mammoth proportions. Sweden itself causes a problem within Scandinavia as it tries to plug the drain of its own best talent to America. Several Swedish companies send inter-

viewers to Finnish technical schools in the middle of a course, and
they may induce as much as eighty per cent of a class to migrate to
Sweden. Today, an estimated 300,000 technology-oriented Finns
(including their families) are working and living in Sweden. This is
almost equal to the Swedish minority in Finland, living there since
the time of the Swedish occupation.

Thorkild Franck, Director of the Danish Council for Scientific
and Industrial Research, estimates that some ten per cent of the
young engineers graduating from Danish universities leave to work
abroad, and Sweden accounts for a great deal of the intake. This

TABLE II

One Year's Net Balance of Graduate Migration Affecting Sweden [1]

Countries	University Graduates	Ph.D. Level	Field of Specialization
Denmark	+42	−1	medicine, technology
Norway	+12 or 13	−1 or 2	technology
Finland	+20	+4	all fields
Iceland	+ 5	—	medicine
France	− 6 or 7	−1	economics, science, technology
Switzerland	−18 or 19	−4	economics, science, law
Italy	− 5 or 6	−1 or 2	humanities
Spain	− 6 or 7	—	technology, humanities
Great Britain	−10	—	technology, humanities
Germany	+ 9	+3	medicine, technology, humanities
Hungary	+20 or 21	—	technology, medicine
Austria	+18	+7	medicine, technology
USA	−24 or 25	+1	science, law, technology
Canada	+ 1 or 2	+1	technology
Australia	− 1 or 2	—	technology
Africa	− 4 or 5	−1	technology, economics
Asia	− 3	—	technology
South America	− 2	—	technology, economics

[1] By Göran Friborg

drain is really an expression in human terms of a gap between two kinds of opportunities. The current brain drain from Denmark to Sweden has put the Danish industries two or three years behind the Swedes, and if the drain continues the gap will increase.

Superficially the Scandinavian drain may look as if it were due solely to a difference in salaries.[1] Informed opinion suggests that this is not the case. The same reason has been given for the drain from Europe to the U.S.A. Let us consider, for example, just what American salaries are worth compared to European ones. To do this we must take into account the taxation at different levels of income, and the comparative cost of living between the different countries.[2]

First, we will concern ourselves with a direct comparison of gross salaries. A man earning £5000 a year in Britain would probably earn, in America, for an equal job and status, £9430; in France, £7570; in Belgium, £6700; in Italy, £6800; in Sweden, £7670; and in Germany, £6500. It can be seen at a glance that, at this level, British executives are poorly paid.

Comparison of starting salaries for graduates shows an even larger disparity. The United States College Placement Council's 1967 report showed the average starting salary for new graduates as just over $8500 (about £3500), ranging from $7600 for physics and chemistry graduates to $9400 for mechanical engineers.[3] Men with Master's degrees start beyond $10,000, and those holding Doctorates can easily start beyond $15,000. The corresponding salaries in Britain are about £1000 for a B.Sc., £1100 for an M.Sc. and a probable maximum of £1500 for a Ph.D. The graduate in Britain is therefore paid less than one-third the salary of an American graduate.

[1] A Danish M.D. going to work in Sweden, for example, can easily get a twenty per cent increase.
[2] We are greatly helped in this job by the report published in 1968 by Associated Industrial Consultants, who conducted a survey of the conditions of executives in several countries. We have also drawn freely from other sources. It is of course impossible to be precise about cost of living differentials, but A.I.C. took an aggregate of previous reliable reports.
[3] Better still, some of our B.Sc. graduates at Washington State University, in 1967, with major in Information Science, received industry offers of $12,000.

After taxation, the picture becomes worse. It is only recently that various investigations have revealed how the British burden of taxation affects take-home pay. A.I.C., for one, gave the figures presented in Table III for retained income, based on income for a married man with two children.

TABLE III

What's Left After Tax in £s

Married man with two children with tax levels at Sept. 1, 1967

Gross salary	UK	USA	Canada	W. Germany	France
2000	1637	1846	1900	1779	1930
2200	1773	2015	2010	1941	2115
2600	2045	2350	2310	2258	2430
3000	2317	2680	2600	2564	2770
4000	2996	3485	3360	3266	3645
5000	3629	4275	4050	3922	4420
7500	4947	6180	5550	5380	6295
10,000	5973	8010	6935	6780	8080

According to the scale in Table III the percentages of income retained are, at £2000:

UK	82
W. Germany	89
USA	92
Canada	95
France	97

And at £5000:

UK	73
W. Germany	78
Canada	81
USA	86
France	89

A direct comparison between Britain and America, at the salary levels of £2000, £5000, £7500 and £10,000 shows the following percentages of income retained after tax:

	£2000	£5000	£7500	£10,000
Britain	82	73	66	60
America	92	86	82	80

At virtually every level above £2000 Britain is taxed more heavily than any of the leading Western nations, and as the salary scale rises so does the disparity in retained income. The disparity at the lower levels is not quite as great as many people had assumed, but this hardly interests the trained scientist. Only when we take a look at the cost of living indices is the disparity somewhat reduced.

After investigating three different cost of living indices (the UN, the *Financial Times* survey, and the Wiesbaden Index) A.I.C. gave the following comparison: [1]

London	100
New York	158
Stockholm	147·5
Paris	139
Geneva	134
Montreal	131
Copenhagen	117·5
The Hague	110
Düsseldorf/Bonn	110
Vienna	107·5
Madrid	106

In an article in its November 1967 issue, *Management Today* stated that taking income tax and cost of living into consideration, British managers earning less than £4000 were not badly paid compared with their continental colleagues, but the difference was marked at the higher salary levels. The thesis would seem to emerge that at the lower salary levels, it is the absolute low pay rather than the high tax which puts Britons at a disadvantage with their continental and American counterparts; at the higher levels it is both the low pay and the high tax which is biting.

America leads all European nations except France and Portugal in the amount of retained income at any salary level, and in these two countries the effect is offset elsewhere: in France by the high

[1] One should remember however that a capital city is *not* generally representative of its country, so far as cost of living is concerned.

cost of living represented by *indirect* taxation, and in Portugal by the low salaries in absolute terms.

For Britain at least, a decrease in direct taxation at the higher level should be considered an inseparable part of any Government initiative to strike at the financial causes of the brain drain. Most ambitious young Ph.D.s in science and engineering set their sights at considerably more than £2000 per annum and are well aware of the inroads that UK taxation would make on their earnings. It is quite horrifying to read the conclusions of the Jones Report [1] in this respect:

'Let us suppose that the aspirations of an engineer are to achieve the standard of living represented by £5000 net in the United Kingdom (and say $15,000 net in the United States) by the time he reaches his mid-forties and has had about twenty-two years' experience. On our stated assumptions, he would need to earn £7650 gross in the United Kingdom, and $18,450 in the United States. According to the latest (1966) surveys of engineering salaries his chances of reaching this level in the United Kingdom are less than one in 200. In the United States they are one in four.'

In a perceptive article, A. J. Merrett [2] advanced the bold theory that the total of future tax revenues lost each year by emigration is over twice all the money collected by surtax. He said it was four times the taxation probably obtained from surtax on earned incomes, and a forty per cent cut in surtax on earned incomes would pay for itself if it only kept in the country one in ten potential emigrants.

Of course, young scientists contemplating a personal contribution to the brain drain must consider not only retained salary levels and nominal cost of living but also the other expensive requirements to which the European will be obliged to adapt himself. It is these

[1] *The Brain Drain: Report of the Working Group on Migration*, presented to Parliament in October 1967 by the Secretary of State for Education and Science and the Minister of Technology. Dr F. E. Jones was chairman of the Working Group.

[2] *Management Today*, December 1967.

which are fairly costly in the US—and they cannot, as in Europe, be separated from the working life. Americans expect that a man's job status will be reflected by his choice of car, living area and, sometimes, wife; and promotion depends on conformity to this rule.

Let us take an example. A German scientist working with a major American corporation was once told by his immediate supervisor to provide his wife with a real mink coat, of the sort possessed by the wives of the other executives. Without such status symbols men are excluded from social events to a degree detrimental to their career. However, it cannot be claimed with certainty that the purchase of obligatory status symbols makes for a substantially higher cost of living than in Europe. The Earl of Kilmuir was perfectly right when he said in a parliamentary debate that the European scientist emigrating to America had some fifty per cent more spending power. To what degree this spending power is consumed by the annual change in car model, the wife's mink coat and the choice of holiday sites is debatable.

Another serious concern of the prospective immigrant to America is the possibility of conscription to the armed forces. An American recruiting campaign recorded that, second to concern about the job, the threat of call-up to military service in Vietnam was the biggest deterrent to emigration to America. The American authorities can sometimes be elusive on this point but the facts are that every emigrant to America born on or after September 15, 1925 is obliged to register himself with the local Selection Service Bureau after six months' residence in the United States, and is then liable for military service. If, however, a man has a record of prior service for an American ally, this may be considered as equivalent to service for America.

The liability to call-up, serious as it may be today, is temporary and in no way constitutes solid material for European planners. This liability can be affected by age, health and marital status. The rules can vary slightly from state to state. There is also consideration for the importance of the immigrant's job; a man working on a government research project is more likely to have his call-up deferred than one working, for instance, in retailing.

The British taxation system has been the object of considerable criticism as a direct contribution to the brain drain. Income tax has reached such a high level that it has become virtually impossible for an individual, however valuable his contribution to the community, to be given adequate incentives or rewards for his efforts. In this light, financial conditions in America and Canada are very favourable, for not only does a man earn more in real terms, but due to milder taxation he sees more of this money.

British management has been caught in the swinging doors of expediency and pay squeeze. Expediency leads to false judgments, with experience being rated above formal university background. The pay squeeze gives the university graduate a poor man's salary. This neither induces cost/effectiveness and hard work, nor eases the brain drain. In the long run, failure to increase the proportion of university men in British management will have detrimental effects on industry at large. The proportion will never be increased until knowhow is given the appreciation it deserves.

Briefly, the statement can be made that a state of affairs in which the brains of the nation are underpaid and overtaxed should not present any attractions to Britain—or to any country for that matter. But change will not come easily. One of the basic prerequisites for changing things is the will to see change through. Our research has strengthened our belief that without an imaginative 'total approach' to the development and control of a nation's brainpower, one cannot expect (or even hope for) better results.

Chapter Two

THE MOBILITY OF THE
BRAIN POWER

'I'd rather be right than consistent. During a
long life I have had to eat my own words many
times, and I have found them a very nourishing
diet.'   Lord Alanbrook

Modern transportation, cheaper power and an automation-assisted
labour force have largely freed industry from its former need for
location close to mines, markets or seaports. In a similar manner,
the evolving conditions of society are freeing men from communities
and nations towards which they have felt bonds of loyalty in the
past. The cutting edge of technology has added a new dimension to
the structure which dominated human relations in years past.

It has been argued that a country invests enough in a man's
growth, career and well-being to expect a certain gratitude in return. But what is really meant by 'gratitude'? Does this mean that
a man should sacrifice his career, his dreams, his professional horizons? What a trained man can contribute is his inventory of intelligence in scientific investigation and in economic management.
Ironically, that is exactly the contribution which is not asked of
him.

The issue of 'reserves of intelligence' dramatizes the bottleneck
in the social and industrial systems in Western Europe today. Because they leave untapped their greatest resource, 'men', these
systems have been starved of thought as well as of funds in recent
years. The whole question of the cost of the brain drain to the
countries suffering it is discussed in Chapter Four, but let us take

a quick look now at what the cost is to Britain of training a man to B.Sc. or Ph.D. standard and then losing him.

First, it has been estimated that in Britain the cost of educating (after minimum school-leaving age) a typical B.Sc. in engineering is £6000, and a Ph.D. in physics is £16,000. This should be regarded as an investment in Britain's economic future similar to the cost of capital expenditure in buildings, machinery and laboratories. To this we must add the value of the emigrant's working life in Britain which is minimally expressed by the value an employer would have placed on him. His salary from graduation to retirement might be £100,000 and could be very much more.

Professor H. Johnson, the Canadian economist, has said that a further loss caused by emigration is the lost opportunity to recoup by taxation some of the cost of the emigrant's education. For good measure we must throw in the value of any invention beneficial to the society that the emigrant might have made, and we begin to appreciate that Britain has lost and continues to lose very considerable assets.

It seems obvious that the Government should protect its investment by offering salaries and conditions which equate fairly with the scientist's value. No government can expect loyalty unless it is prepared to demonstrate its own loyalty by offering adequate rewards for work and achievement.

Many people in Europe feel strongly that since a nation's citizens have paid, through taxation, for sixteen or seventeen years of education of the new generation, young men and women have an obligation to repay the debt by service of a limited number of years to their own country. Many countries do place some restriction on the movement of their graduates overseas, especially the new developing countries. Conditions of government service are attached to overseas scholarships. The scientific adviser to the Indian High Commissioner in London, Mr Kidwai, asserts that education is an investment and a country has the right to reap the benefits. In Ceylon every graduate is contractually bound to serve the government for five years. And in Egypt engineering graduates are not allowed to leave the country for fifteen years.

But it would be much more difficult to apply this logic to European conditions, especially while we are at the stage of trying to break down feelings of rigid nationalism (read: provincialism) in the old continent. Such restrictions fly in the face of many of our traditions and political beliefs. They are, moreover, unworkable in any but a short-term context. India, Ceylon and Egypt are in a different situation—they need all the brain power they can produce. Europe apparently does not need all she produces or she would be employing it instead of suffering a brain drain. It is obviously pointless to overproduce talent and then confine it where it can only be driven to frustration.

The men at the steering-wheels of the different European governments must on the one hand recognize that brainpower is the vital force behind progress; on the other, they must be realistic enough to appreciate that no valid solution can be found by producing brainpower to which adequate (and imaginative) employment is denied.

The degree of loyalty required appears to be variable. It seems to be widely felt (probably largely for emotional reasons) that those men and women who have been trained in the medical profession have a greater debt of loyalty to their country than almost any other members of society. Yet the migration of doctors to the United States continues to increase. A survey made by the Junior Hospital Doctors Association early in 1967 showed that almost half the junior doctors in Britain were at that time considering emigration. The reasons were given as utter dissatisfaction with pay, conditions and training facilities. The actual emigration rate among junior hospital doctors has been between 350 and 400 per annum, that is 22–25 per cent of annual output, and accounts for about a third of America's immigrant doctors.

In September 1966, some six hundred doctors sat for an examination in London that would help them qualify to practise medicine in the United States, and the Ministry of Health promptly made an attack on doctors who leave Britain. It accused them of being 'cynical and selfish', since it cost the British taxpayer an estimated 7000 guineas per man to train each one.

All those who take the test are not, however, of British nationality. More than half are Indians or Pakistanis who themselves have moved to Britain for the same basic reasons that cause some 300 to 400 British doctors to leave each year for the United States. To accuse intending emigrants of being cynical and selfish is not the way to halt the brain drain. It certainly did not prevent a further 800 doctors taking a similar examination early the following year.

Let nobody be fooled by references to the 'reverse brain drain'. The reversal of a rooted trend calls for bold acts, not for more words. While it is good news to hear that ICI 'recently brought across a group of American science graduates', and that 'other firms are doing the same thing', we must not allow ourselves to be mesmerized by such statements. The numbers are too small to indicate a trend, let alone a reversal. Nor is the initiative of one or two firms enough to provide the needed thrust.

It is the government which has an obligation to ensure that a country's human resources are not dissipated. This is where the question of loyalty starts and finishes. The government, through thoughtful action, must ensure that human resources are used in the proper manner and that each engineer, scientist, doctor or manager gets both the opportunities and the rewards he deserves. What a man owes to the country which trains him can only be judged in the light of his government's attitude to him afterwards. Loyalty must work reciprocally.

We can conclude, therefore, that while a man may feel obliged, to some extent, to repay his country of origin, in terms of service, for his training, this is not the only direction in which a man's loyalties should lie. He has a responsibility for himself and, if married, for his wife and family. Further, he can feel quite justified in expecting from his country a return for his services in the way of financial rewards, career opportunities and personal development. No relationship can be fully successful if it is one-sided, and there must be constant give and take. That is why we cannot condemn as 'unethical' a man who is prepared to go where the opportunities are greatest.

It is becoming clear that industry by itself cannot stop the brain drain. What is required is the scope for talent which only government can create. The international facts of life must be accepted, and massive financial support given to Research and Development. Success of such a policy would depend on the universities' capacity to produce the scientists which industry would need, and that in turn would call for comprehensive and long-term planning between government, university and industry. No government in Europe has yet accepted this challenge and it will soon be too late to make a start.

The inadequacy of stop-gap measures was exposed in Sweden in 1964 in what has come to be known as the Hörmander case. The distinguished mathematician caused alarm by saying he had been invited by Princeton's Institute of Advanced Studies to accept a chair as Research Professor. Lund University, in an attempt to retain Hörmander's services in Sweden, thereupon created a research professorship which Hörmander was prepared to accept. But the law of the land did not allow such deviation from the traditions of the Middle Ages. The chair was not created and Hörmander left for Princeton. After a public outcry a law was introduced to stop further loss of high calibre men by allowing universities to create research professorships for prominent engineers, mathematicians and scientists. It was too late to help Hörmander but was successfully applied to another mathematician in 1966.

Much is wrong with the way Europe's science and technology is developing. As Dr Karl-Olof Faxén[1] has pointed out, the brain drain is unavoidable as long as European countries hesitate to take the risks of change. 'Security,' he said, 'is the worst enemy of progress and of variation. Yet, our strategy in Europe today is

[1] Director, Research Department, Swedish Employers' Association.

based more on security than on anything else.' By burying progress and closing eyes to the future, a continent cannot be developed.

Security has for too long been at the top of the list of human prerequisites. In most countries men still look for security in immobility, the sort of immobility-security characterized in international terms in the 1930s by the Maginot Line. But immobility is not security, it is stagnation. And besides, security is the coin which should be spent when needed.

Mobility is another matter for consideration. In Britain there is a distinct reluctance in men to move away from London, and it is often easier to persuade a graduate and his family to move to America than to the north of England. American men show a far greater willingness to move from state to state, though in America too there is a general drift towards California. If Britain is to induce increased mobility of graduates within her boundaries, she must not only re-educate them to understand the importance of mobility, but create in other industrial centres the attractions of London.

Sometimes governments can appear even more reticent about the need for mobility than individuals, and shrink from creating the required professional and environmental conditions to encourage movement between the industrial centres of their country.

What we said about geographic mobility applies to management mobility as well. With expanding job opportunities, mobility is no longer considered unethical, a sort of executive 'vagabondage'. Indeed, quite the opposite happens to be the case. Stagnation in management mutation will bring about a freeze in management evolution, leading to a painful professional retrenchment.

A study by the French Institute for Statistics and Economic Studies indicated that over a five-year period (1960–64) more than four million Frenchmen, or almost one working person in five, had their professional status modified: a transition from wage-earning to salaried status, or movement between technical and managerial posts, etc. The younger people had been the most exposed to change, for almost half the number involved were under thirty-five years of age.

According to the French statistics, men have been much more mobile than women, and movement has been greater within the industrial and professional sectors, or those which require unskilled labour over long stretches of time. In this way, the textile, garment, leather and building industries have registered the highest losses in personnel to the benefit of the mechanical and electrical industries. In contrast, some of these industries, such as public works and building, have gained unskilled labour from other declining industries, agriculture and mining being two examples.

Mutations are thus happening at the lower levels but not among men of a higher professional status. Thus it should come as no surprise that as of January 1968 an estimated 25,000 French 'cadres' (professional men, university graduates, management level employees) were unemployed. Most of them had failed to develop their skills and they were cropped out as merging companies coolly eliminated those managers who were simply creating work for one another.

Moreover, solutions will not create themselves. Without imaginative and bold action, five years from now we will be saying: 'How did we ever get trapped into another vicious cycle?' Only when European governments are prepared to unite their research outlays in a far-sighted programme might they have a chance of catching up with America. European nations must guard against thinking that they can buy a ticket into the future at bargain prices. The ever-widening technological gap between America and Europe is the result of that illusion, and the gap may be beyond repair.

These last points are, of course, intimately connected with the issue of professional opportunity. European and American companies are definitely not in the same class as far as research outlays are concerned. European researchers fall hungrily on the few, inadequate crumbs that governments are prepared to offer in the way of financial support for their projects. But surely industries need more sustenance than this if they are to survive. Wishful thinking will not make up the difference, and it cannot be repeated too often that there is no alternative to an integrated pan-European approach to science and industry.

Amadeo Peter Giannini, a Genoese immigrant's son, would not have been able to find in Italy the grounds on which to build his Bank of America but he might have had a chance of finding them in an economically, industrially and socially united Europe. The Bank of America is now the largest bank in the world, with assets of nearly $18 billion, more than the combined gross national products of Ireland, Israel and Norway.

Dr Friedrich Hämmerling[1] has given another excellent example of Europe's plight; an example that dramatizes European industry's disadvantage in being supported by an understructure of inadequate breadth and weight. Said he: 'The stock market value of IBM is today greater than the integrated value of the whole of German industry.'

On December 29, 1966, Paul Henri Spaak, speaking on 'European Discord', in the House of Europe, Nice, said that the current political scene throughout Europe appeared completely opposed to the idea of a united effort, and industrial, economic, technological and political unity was being sacrificed on the altar of national sovereignty.

'The existence of the nation is as disputable and perishable as any other man-made concept. The very idea of a nation has been forged over a number of centuries but nobody can ever be certain that this is the ultimate in evolution and that growth and survival will not lead to larger units.'

Spaak's views coincide with those expressed by most enlightened men in the course of our research. 'Tribes and nations,' as Konrad Lorenz was to say, 'are pseudospecies.' Beneath the superficial show of declaring the superiority of a race or nation is much unfounded prejudice. Where, then, does the responsibility of the scientist lie

---

[1] Director of Research and Development, and Member of the Board, AEG-Telefunken.

in the matter of national and racial differences? Unhappily for mankind, science is caught between loyalty to the present state and responsibility for its future. Most European governments are caught on the same horns—but not because of science, because of obsolescence.

In discussing the chances of European survival, M. Spaak rightly stated that political integration should precede economic integration.

'I do not believe it is possible to integrate the economics of six nations if each one of them follows an international policy different to that of his neighbour. I do not think that the Common Market can survive if one of its members is the ally of Russia, another one of America, while their partners remain neutral.'

Where the industries of European nations have occasionally got together the effort has often failed through lack of funds. Euratom was said (in January 1967) to have run short of cash and to be living on a day-to-day basis. The European Space Research Organization appears to be in a perpetual state of stress that could have serious political repercussions. The European Launcher Development Organization has had similar crises which can totally demoralize scientists from many European countries. As Lord Windelsham aptly said: 'The abrupt cancellation of major projects, TSR 2 is an example, disrupts whole teams and fragments the knowledge they have built up.'

Amidst the chaotic conditions characterizing the ELDO-ESRO ventures, some lessons can be discerned. The initial intentions ranged from 'simply getting something started' to the real wish to push ahead European space technology. But because of mismanagement (at all levels: from governmental to organizational) not only did the test fail, but the endeavours became diametrically opposed to even the most conservative planner's wishes.

In April 1968 Italy was credited with having pulled the rug from under the feet of ESRO—and Britain with having done just the same for the ELDO side. By withdrawing from ESRO, Italy killed the most promising projects of that organization: two heavy satellites—forerunners of a European telecommunications satellite. Matra, a French company, was awarded the systems responsibility —and Italy was expected to pay for French research, which it refused to do.

As for ELDO, Britain simply announced that it would not renew its membership when the multinational agreement expires in 1972.[1] The regional TV communications satellite fell with the same blow. This communications satellite was intended to provide a means for relaying TV programmes among the members of the European Broadcasting Union. As the smoke clears, European technology is doubly hurt: both in research and in morale.

The European technologists who have been saying that a new head of government here or there would improve things are wrong on at least one count. They are like the sailors in the storm who thought the appointment of another captain would make the wind stop blowing. The dice are loaded against technology and science in Europe unless we decide to stop the farce. This calls for a greater change in hearts than many men imagine. It calls for a true, not pseudo, Knowledge Revolution.

[1] The British were known to be unhappy about rising costs, especially since Britain was footing twenty-seven per cent of the bill.

Chapter Three

THE HIDDEN BRAIN DRAIN

'The idea of progress could not have become part
of general thought until men could see that, in
one respect or another, they were improving
their lot.'   Julian Huxley

One of the dangers of the brain drain is that it is immeasurable.
It has many outlets, and one of them is what we shall refer to as the
'hidden brain drain'. Its existence has been discussed on certain
occasions but its extent and impact have never been appreciated
as they should.

The hidden drain consists of engineers, technologists and scientists working in their country of origin but for a foreign company.
It also includes high-level managers in the same position. Research
and development centres sponsored, financed and controlled by
American corporations in England, France, Germany, Italy, Sweden,
Switzerland and nearly every other Western European country
form an integral part of the hidden brain drain. Take for instance
IBM laboratories working on computers and terminal units for data
processing equipment: the original idea and the original design
for the 1401 came from their laboratories set up in, and largely
staffed from, France and Germany; the high speed printer (1200
lpm) from the IBM laboratories in Japan.

A similar case is that of Lockheed, who have established themselves in London to employ those British aeronautical scientists
who expressedly did not wish to emigrate to the United States
yet were virtually unemployed as a result of the cancellation of
the TSR 2. For Lockheed, they will now help with the design of
the supercargo C-5A. Eventually, the ability to tap the resources

in brain power wherever they exist will be the greatest single factor characterizing a growth company.

At least two executive search companies, Anonymous Appointments and Premmit, are persuading American companies to set up research and development centres in the UK. They believe it is unrealistic and uneconomic to attempt to reverse the geographical brain drain from Europe to America, not because there are insufficient numbers of scientists and technologists who would prefer to work in Europe than America (the reverse is the case) but because of the unwillingness of British companies to employ them. Either the British firms have no employment vacancies in their existing organizations, or they are not prepared to pay the salaries that men with university backgrounds and years of experience have learned to consider reasonable.

Both firms have tried to place scientists and engineers who desired to return, but without any success. Out of about twenty candidates of British origin, Premmit could not place a single one in British industry. Anonymous Appointments collected the names of 200 Ph.D.s, most of them British, but similarly found that British companies were just not interested. And both firms believe that the idea of American R & D centres in Britain will give British scientists the latest research problems to solve, and the most interesting work to do, which at present is mainly to be found in American industry.

Angus Douglass,[1] who can be regarded as a professional brain gainer for America, recommends Europe to set up research centres on the American pattern. These centres could be commissioned for the sort of research work that European scientists are already doing, but for American companies in America. This solution would keep the brains in England and earn dollars from American industry. It must be remembered that the basic requirement is not the physical presence of brains in Europe but the opportunity to market the products of those brains as *European* products.

The host country often appreciates the sort of R & D push it

[1] President of the American recruiting organization Careers Inc.

gets. Ford Motor Company's research and engineering centre in Essex was officially opened by the British Prime Minister in October 1967. More than 3500 engineers, technologists, scientists and other staff have been brought together to work on problems of motor vehicle design. Ford's chairman claims that the company has invested £10 million in the project. Admittedly, few firms in Europe could afford to initiate research projects of the required magnitude, and even £10 million is not particularly impressive compared with the research outlays of some American companies at home.

The trouble with the hidden brain drain is that such centres of research not only attract the best talents, they also neutralize them as far as advances by European companies are concerned. And besides, while such centres may well keep English scientists and technologists aware of progress in America, the men working for American companies are also inevitably aware of any interesting new developments in British private or governmental laboratories— which gives the hidden brain drain an extra dimension.

The hidden brain drain is particularly worrying because one of the greatest qualities of American industry (as we shall discuss in the last chapter) is its ability to move very quickly from the laboratory to the production line. Hence, too many good ideas are going abroad for alien development and its resultant competitive advantage. If the conventional brain drain slows down or is restricted through legislation, the hidden brain drain will probably increase. And 'guestimates' say that the hidden brain drain is already larger than the more obvious migratory one: one estimation has put it two and a half times as high.

The hidden brain drain throws up some tantalizing questions. If it is admitted that a brain drain of a certain level is unavoidable, it is also reasonable to ask whether the 'hidden' variety might not be better than the migratory one. The answer is complex because one must bring into the equation the loyalties and motivation of the men involved. It is reasonable for foreign companies operating abroad to expect the loyalty and full support of management. If this is the case, where do men stand in relation to loyalty to their country of origin?

The hidden brain drain presents a conflict of interests and any special plea for national interest could seem to be hypocritical. The problem is not purely an American one. ICI's continental head-quarters in Brussels will have to face it, and Shell and Unilever in the United States who are operating a hidden brain drain in reverse. Most companies of international dimensions will be faced with the question sooner or later. Dr Jones, the chairman of the Working Group on Migration which produced the Jones Report, is also the managing director of Mullard. Mullard is now under Phillips' (hence Dutch) control.

THE SCAPEGOAT THEORY

Facts about the brain drain are often distorted into a 'scapegoat theory' that places total responsibility for Europe's drain of talent on to the evil intentions of America.

During his December 1966 visit to Paris, Russian leader Alexei Kosygin accused the United States of encouraging the brain drain. In his Sorbonne speech he complained that America used its technological advantage to impose its will on others. He then touched on a sensitive point by assuring his audience that there was plenty of opportunity for the trained European at home. 'The theory that the United States is continuing to widen its head-start in scientific and technological fields and that there is nothing for Western Europe to do but let itself be taken over by America is a retrograde notion,' he said.

A fortnight after Mr Kosygin's speech, Lord Bowden[1] described the United States space race and defence programmes as 'scientifically trivial' and designed chiefly to attract ability. Yet, who can say that the attraction of skill and knowhow is not an end in itself? Rather, the ethical aspect of it is in question; and as we have stated, the ethical aspect is multi-phased.

[1] Former Labour Minister of State for Education and Science, and Principal of Manchester College of Science and Technology.

There has been considerable controversy in European countries about the morality of large-scale American advertising of scientific and professional positions. Recent American approaches to European scientists have been dramatic and widespread. A full-page announcement in the British *New Scientist* that 'the Americans are coming', and exhorting scientists to see for themselves what America had to offer, provoked a wealth of unfavourable comment.[1] And while the British Government feels that the restriction of advertising would serve to stimulate discontent, and that the only way to stop the brain drain is to make the United Kingdom a better place for scientists and technologists to work in, in Germany extensive American advertising is banned.

Although large-scale American recruiting campaigns cause the most alarm, there have been more limited schemes which also threaten to increase the proportions of the brain drain. In 1967 the Franklin National Bank, in a recruiting campaign launched in leading British newspapers, advertised for chief clerks in British banks with about ten years' experience to take up positions in America. Mr Scudder Kelvie, a vice president of the bank, was reported as being extremely optimistic about the scheme: 'From what I have heard of the labour market in Britain, the country is somewhat flush with bankers. We are looking for bright young guys who can develop into officers of the bank in a very short time.' This campaign provoked much criticism, especially from the British banks.

William Douglass[2] is quite open about his intentions. As he commented in a *New Scientist* article[3]:

'. . . Simply I plan to continue to sell the excellence of British brains in America while at the same time doing all I can to have your government and industrial leaders see the opportunity this

[1] The advertisement was placed by Careers Incorporated, and interview centres were set up to deal with the response, in London and other major European cities.
[2] Managing director of Careers Incorporated (UK) Ltd.
[3] April 6, 1967.

excellence affords. The only thing wrong with the brain drain is that it is one way. If you had the power, you would do what we are doing yourselves. In fact you are doing so right now. India and Nigeria, to name two, must be feeling unhappy over the way you are taking their doctors.'

So is it realistic to put the blame for the British and continental European losses entirely on America? Unless we attribute to the American government a fiendish plot to hinder Europe's economy we must accept it merely as a case of industrial management purchasing the best ability available, as we would do if we could. It is all too easy to condemn America for being rich pirates of ability but we will never advance from our present position until we create the same opportunities in Europe as in America. Once that is achieved, how many young Europeans would choose to migrate?

The American public dislikes intensely its popular image of the richest country in the world enhancing its position by luring away the potential leaders of the poorer nations, and set up a committee to examine the facts of the situation. This committee concluded that the picture of the rich robbing the poor is highly distorted, and while it has advanced no solution for the brain drain as such, it has been at pains to point out that it is no part of United States Government policy to increase the flow of qualified immigrants.

Dr Donald Hornig[1] spoke very firmly on the American position while giving evidence to a Senate Committee in March 1967. Since he is the President's adviser on scientific matters it is worth quoting him at length.

'If the domestic policies of a number of advanced nations demonstrated nearly the same high evaluation of their scientists and engineers that are evident in their protests over their brain drain, the outward flow would be markedly diminished. I would like to be specific on this point. For example, the relatively low level of investment in higher education in all European countries results not only in fewer opportunities for students but also in fewer faculty

[1] Director of the US Office of Science and Technology.

48

places in universities where talented scientists and engineers can find satisfaction in teaching and in independent research.

'With the exception of a few top professors, the status and range of opportunity of the scientists and engineers are low. In comparison with our tradition and practice, little autonomy is given to junior workers, and the length of time over which they are kept in poorly rewarded positions of low status and scientific opportunity is shocking by our standards. This widespread failure to recognize and encourage the full potential of people has its worst effects precisely in the case of young workers who are at the peak of their potential creativity. It is for the theoretically inclined seeker after truth who is most interested in fundamental research that this difference in opportunity level is greatest. . . .

'In short, one's sympathy for the countries concerned must be balanced by sympathy and understanding for those whose aspirations are blunted by forces over which they have little or no control. The status of engineering and management personnel in many advanced countries is even lower than that of academic scientists. Their influence at top management levels is frequently low. They are often treated as technicians rather than as full participants in the major affairs and major decisions of companies. . . .

'It is misleading to assume either that the brain drain causes the technological gap or that the technological gap causes the brain drain. In my judgment, it is more fruitful to view both of them as consequences of more fundamental factors such as those I have outlined above.

'In short, I do not believe the simple thesis, put forward in some advanced countries, that the United States attracts people simply because it is rich and accepts them because it is insensitive to the needs of others. The issues are much more complex.'

This underlines the issue but does not solve the problem. America is the first to admit her moral responsibilities to the advanced and the developing nations of the world. Less evident is what can be done about the challenge. Another real dilemma for the United States is the attitude she should take towards European nations who, although advanced, have an increasing technological and management gap with the United States.

The low investment level in education leads to a low national status for research workers. As many far-sighted men have already realized, unless the domestic policies of certain advanced nations are geared to the re-evaluation of the nation's scientists and engineers, the brain drain will not only continue, but increase.

Legislation can only be of partial and temporary help. The changes in the United States immigration laws which took effect on July 1, 1968 at first sight appear likely to reduce the brain drain, particularly the drain between Britain and the USA. Before July 1968, every country in the world was allocated an immigrant quota into the United States based on the ethnic make-up of the American population. The effect of this was to give northern European countries very large quotas that were never fully used. Britain, for instance, had a quota of 65,000 immigrants per year which was never more than half used. There was never a British waiting list to enter the USA. Other countries, with small quotas or heavy demand, had enormous waiting lists.

The law which took effect in July 1968 abolished the *national* quota system and substituted a 'first-come, first-served' system on a world-wide preference basis. All immigrants, of whatever origin, are now considered in strict order of application according to the following scale of preferences—which had previously only been applied to countries which overflowed their quotas:

1 Unmarried son or daughter of an American citizen
2 Spouse of alien resident in the United States
3 Professional or highly skilled immigrant
4 Married son or daughter of an American citizen
5 Brother or sister of an American citizen
6 Needed skilled or unskilled worker

At this moment, the likely effect of the new law on the brain drain is highly uncertain. The new legislation[1] appears to have been passed because national quotas were thought to be discriminatory. It was felt that the questions asked of intending immigrants should be not 'Where were you born?' but rather 'What is your present connection with the United States?' or 'What skills do you have to offer?'

As July 1968 approached, many objections to the bill began to be heard in high places in American government. The Chairman of the Judiciary Committee, and the Chairman of the relevant committee in the House of Representatives, were only two who had foreseen the difficulties when the legislation had first been passed. One undesirable effect would be to let in a greater number of Asians and thereby aggravate the drain from underdeveloped countries. Another objection was against the anomaly that discriminated against those countries of northern Europe which had kept their immigration below the level which they were allowed. The American Consul General in London said that free access from Britain to the United States was blocked for the first time in history. But US industry is still actively campaigning to alter the law, and mounting pressure for legislative changes can be expected.

The affect of the legislation on the brain drain will probably not be as great as anticipated anyway. The *hidden* brain drain will obviously increase. More US research centres will be established in Europe. While these centres certainly keep some brains geographically in Europe, the output of those brains benefits the USA, not Europe. It is also fairly certain that ways will be found to dodge the full impact of the new laws. More sophisticated use will be made of non-immigrant visas by US companies anxiously seeking European talent. Economic demands in the United States may well require legislative changes in the order of priority of the scale of preferences—to favour skills. It is most unlikely that the present situation will be static for long.

---

[1] This law was actually passed in November 1965, and it was decided that during the 2½-year interim period, unused quotas should go into a general pool to be used by countries with waiting lists.

Although America is very aware of the advantage she derives from highly-talented immigration, and although American industry can be expected to fight as hard as possible to temper the force of the immigration law as it effects northern Europe, we nevertheless agree with Dr Hornig that the blame for the existing conditions lies with Europe. It is very much a part of the American tradition not to restrict freedom of movement where labour is concerned, but no action of the US Government can be said to have encouraged the brain drain from European and other countries. It lies with Europe to put her own house in order.

At this stage of her economic history, the fact that the brain drain has suddenly been plugged before any provisions have been made for absorbing the resultant overflow, may have harmful and unexpected effects. Unfortunately, theoretical alarm at the exodus of brains from Europe is not matched by practical determination to create European opportunities for them.

Chapter Four

THE PLIGHT OF EUROPE

'The new empires are the empires of the mind.'
Winston Churchill

In early 1966 OECD reported a staggering five per cent brain drain [1] from the continent of Europe, and it is of little consolation that in parts of the world the situation is even worse. Europe loses brains to America while it gains for itself brain power from lesser developed countries. Evidently this does not serve anybody except America.

The underdeveloped countries desperately need the trained men they lose, and Europe badly needs its own trained men who have grown in the European environment and who will generally be more valuable than a graduate of a developing country whose education and professional qualifications will be of a lower standard. That is the irony of the brain drain. For European countries (limited as they happen to be in natural resources) it is a matter of life or death to regain the lead. Like it or not, they have to rely on brainpower for their future.

Probably the most reliable statistics available for Britain's contribution to the brain drain are given in the Jones Report. The figures in Table IV show British and Commonwealth engineers, technologists and scientists going abroad during the period 1961–66 and intending to stay at least one year. While some of these people do return, there are many more who intend to stay only a few years but who eventually settle and become American citizens.

That America is the eventual destination of the vast majority of brain drain emigrants is hardly in question. Almost as many

[1] Of the annual output of university level graduates.

TABLE IV

*Estimated Emigration of British and Commonwealth Engineers,
Technologists and Scientists Going Abroad for a Minimum of One Year*

	Total emigration	Engineers and technologists	Scientists
		(figures rounded to nearest 100)	
1961	3200	1900	1300
1962	3500	2200	1300
1963	4000	2500	1500
1964	4700	3100	1700
1965	5100	3300	1800
1966	6200	4200	2000

Source: Ministry of Technology

depart direct to America as to all other countries put together; and although Canada attracts a good number, it is often acting as an unwilling 'staging post' for the journey to the States. Table V, also taken from the Jones Report, shows the number of engineers, technologists and scientists emigrating direct to America as against those emigrating to all other countries, during the period 1961–66.

Between 1961 and 1966 72,000 Europeans, classified as 'professional, technical and kindred workers', entered the United States as immigrants. By far the largest number was from Britain, 23,000 as against the second largest, from Germany, 11,000. Though there was a general fall throughout Europe for the period 1962–66 as against the previous five-year period, Britain's share of the talented emigration rose by more than a quarter. Between June 1965 and June 1966 3900 'professional, technical and kindred workers' entered America from Britain.

Between 1959 and 1961 over 43,000 scientists and engineers migrated to America, many of them from developing countries. A hundred thousand scientists, doctors and engineers not trained in America are now working there, about 15,000 of them from Britain. The value of their training, paid for entirely by their countries of origin, has been estimated at $4000 million. Their services to American industry are probably worth many times that figure. To produce all the doctors it currently receives through

TABLE V

Destinations of British and Commonwealth Engineers, Technologists and Scientists emigrating in the years 1961–1966

	Total	North America	Other countries (figures rounded to nearest 100)
Engineers and technologists			
1961	1900	500	1400
1962	2200	700	1600
1963	2500	800	1700
1964	3100	1000	2100
1965	3300	1300	1900
1966	4200	2000	2200
Scientists			
1961	1300	800	500
1962	1300	800	500
1963	1500	900	600
1964	1700	1000	700
1965	1800	1000	800
1966	2000	1100	900

Source: Ministry of Technology

immigration the United States would have to build twelve new medical schools and run them to capacity each year.

Professor Richard M. Titmuss of the London School of Economics has stated bluntly:

'Since 1949 the United States has absorbed—and to some extent deliberately recruited—100,000 doctors, scientists and engineers from developed and developing countries . . . It has spent more on consumption goods, less on public services. It has taxed itself more lightly while imposing heavier taxation on poorer countries. . . . In medicine alone, foreign doctors now account for nearly twenty per cent of annual additions to the US medical profession. The world now provides as much or more medical aid to the US in terms of dollars as the total cost of all American medical aid, private and public, to foreign countries.'

What we must continually stress throughout this survey is the quality of the people who leave, not merely the quantity. If 15,000 dustmen left Britain for the United States it would pose a considerable temporary problem but one imagines that a further 15,000 dustmen would be fairly quickly obtainable. But 15,000 doctors, scientists and engineers crossing the Atlantic represent, at the very least, 60,000 man-years permanently lost to these vital professions. For every B.A. who goes it takes three to four years to replace him; for every Ph.D., at least seven years.

More than fifteen per cent of men and women taking their Ph.D. each year in Britain emigrate immediately, and usually for the rest of their working lives even if that is not their intention when they depart. Between 1957 and 1962 Britain even lost nine Fellows of the Royal Society. Let us look at a few figures from America's point of view. The equivalent of the Royal Society is the American Academy of Sciences. No less than twenty-four per cent of its current membership graduated abroad. Forty-three American citizens have won Nobel Prizes in physics and chemistry; over one-third of these graduated abroad. In 1963 America received, at no cost to herself, more engineers, physicians and scientists than the total number of first degree scientists and engineers produced by all the universities in Britain.

Even the guess that estimated US savings in training costs alone have been $4000 million may be an underestimate. Mr George Henderson[1] has suggested that the value of the immigrants' output is 'as great or greater than the total of our foreign aid since 1949'. And yet, according to A. J. Merrett writing in *Management Today*, these figures touch only the fringe of the total immigration problem. The Jones Report estimated that the emigrating engineers, technologists and scientists in 1966 numbered 6200 but this is only a fraction of Britain's total emigration and some of this total is only less valuable by degree. Taking only 'skilled and professional emigrants to America, Canada and Australia alone', the number is 40,534, over six times as many as considered in the Jones Report.

While England has lost and continues to lose the most talent in

[1] American Institute for Training and Research.

absolute figures, other European countries are not far behind. Switzerland can claim the dubious distinction of exceeding England's figure as a proportion of her population. And we have spoken of Scandinavia's own internal brain drain which superimposes itself on the pull exercised by America.

The reasons, we said, are generic. Most of the European laboratories suffer from ageing equipment, static horizons, myopic management and starvation budgets. This is a statement of fact and needs no further discussion. Twenty years ago no one could have imagined such a state of affairs. As the leading countries talk about the staggering cost of research and their supposed inability to make ends meet, they induce in their scientific community a reaction of anger and despair. Which is to come first for Europe, the cart or the horse? How is European industry to adapt to the requirements of today and keep its talent from drifting to America?

And while European governments sit and talk but do not think imaginatively about it, the brain drain is accelerating. If anyone attempts to console himself with the knowledge that the total emigration is only a small proportion of available talent, let him bear in mind that, of the emigrants, a large proportion are the best young brains available. They do not leave to seek easier opportunities, but more challenging ones. In this respect it is less of a brain drain than an overflow of cream.

Even the large industries themselves fail to recognize the danger building up before them. Any individual company would only lose perhaps two or three top-level men each year, a tiny proportion of their total staff and a gap easy to refill. But refill with what? You can plug a stone wall with earth but you have weakened the wall, and the chances are that when you have been plugging it for ten years you have a wall built of mud.

If our European industries were much more concentrated the danger would be realized more quickly, but so long as the brain drain is seen by Europe's proliferation of small companies as the loss of two or three men per year, only a few enlightened industrialists will be able to grasp what is happening before their eyes.

We therefore see it as a matter of urgency for the governments of each European country to initiate a study of brain drain and brain gain during the last ten years, and to arrange for regular and comprehensive statistics of emigration of qualified people to be issued yearly. It is important not only to be aware that Mr A. has left for America and Mr B. has arrived from India, but to know enough of their personal and professional motives gradually to build up a comprehensive picture of drain and gain as it affects Europe. It will then be necessary to ensure that industry is informed of the result. Our guess is that their apathy might then disappear.

THE KNOWLEDGE GAP

While the points we have made above stress the scientific and technological loss incurred by European nations as a result of the brain drain, we must not lose sight of the broader picture of the 'knowledge gap'. The effects of the brain drain permeate all levels of our schools, universities, and social and cultural environment. History demonstrates that where a country enjoys a political or scientific or military supremacy over a number of years it invariably coincides with a cultural peak of achievement; Athens and Elizabethan England are only two examples from a long list.

Nations (through university and industry) should guard against any widening of the knowledge gap. We cannot emphasize too often the growing dangers of personnel obsolescence in government, business and industry, as a result of the rapid expansion in human knowledge and technological progress. Each of us is more ignorant now than we were a few years ago because, although we may have added to our personal knowledge in recent years, the world's knowledge has increased infinitely more in proportion: we know less of what there is to know year by year.

Advances in technology tend to upset management standards. Failure to keep up the pace through retooling (by means of executive development programmes) is the best way to dissipate the effectiveness of management, and organizations which lack a sense of vision will build up a feeling of frustration which causes their good executives to leave and the bad ones to hang on like leeches!

When a prospective employee in science, technology or advanced management joins an organization it must present to him an image which fulfils the man's fullest ambitions. Money is important but is secondary to the challenge of the job, the opportunity to be creative and the genuine chance of showing what he can do. And the higher the education of the man, the less he is likely to be content with a job that does not entitle him to the opportunities that competitive positions abroad would offer. But this sort of challenge is one which only a handful of European companies have equipped themselves to offer, and in this respect size is not the main criterion.

It is astonishing that companies which hesitate for months over a choice of automatic coffee machine, weighing efficiency against cost, will casually employ people without any idea of the future path they wish them to follow. A man is chosen against arbitrary criteria such as the kind of school he attended, or, worse yet, whether he is a relative of one of the directors, on the assumption that if he does the industrial apprentice's job well he will eventually make a good manager. Ten years and perhaps £20,000 later they discover he is a bad manager and is still doing—at the management level—the quality of the work he did on entering the company which could be done by any beginner at a starting salary.

Few firms will recognize themselves from this description but will probably have no difficulty in recognizing some of their rivals. But how many companies who smile at that description actually operate a management policy, recruiting with a man's whole career in mind, recognizing that a brilliant physicist may be a bad manager of other people's talent and programming his career accordingly, and actually teaching the job of management rather than assuming that it accumulates with time, like dust?

To put the question from the viewpoint of the employee, how many of them know what they are working towards, in what areas of their work they are weakest, and whether they are on the management or technical ladder? A position on the technical ladder is not an indication of failure, although it is often wrongly so regarded.

We would earnestly advise companies to recognize the invest-ment made when they employ a graduate at £1000+ per year,[1] and service him at least as often as the coffee machine. This in itself would go a long way to solving a company's personnel prob-lems. But by itself it could not stop Europe's brain drain. The extent of planning required by the Knowledge Revolution must be undertaken not only at government level but, ideally, at pan-European level.

It is already too late for small-scale changes in Europe. Europe's prospects for the future are that her science-based industries will become more and more exposed to the biting winds of competition from increasingly efficient American industries. The counterattack must be imaginative.

Within this perspective, the issue of science-intensive industries based on new products should be given particular attention. When a new company is formed, it is recognized that new venture capital is needed, and nobody expects substantial profits immediately. In contrast, a company that has suffered a setback (as most European companies have) is not given the same leniency. People judge that this company has lived long enough to know what it is doing and it is expected to produce profits. However, industries operating at the frontiers of knowledge no longer have (in any absolute sense) the advantages of this accumulated knowledge of the past. And neither, with their restricted European horizons and budgets, do they have the advantages offered by the future. Even Siemens, one of the colossal companies by European standards, found it difficult to raise in the German capital market the money it needed for expansion purposes in mid-1966.

We therefore believe that an important first step towards re-programming European industry is, by amalgamation of separate companies, to build some five pan-European companies each specializing in one of the advanced technology fields: aerospace, computers, components, nuclear plants, oceanography. These

[1] We would have liked to say at £2000 per year, but we have to recognize realities.

pan-European organizations should be allotted annual research budgets just as the Atomic Energy Commissions have their budgets for elaborate technical research, and be totally owned by private investment, compulsory investment if necessary (see below).

Five basic rules should be observed in the structuring of these pan-European corporations:

1 They should operate in every way like comparable private companies of the more traditional nature
2 They should be profit-oriented and profit-minded. Their management should stand or fall on their ability
3 They should adhere rigidly to their prescribed field of manufacture.
4 No intervention in the functioning of the companies by the separate governments should be tolerated
5 Borrowing in the open market should be the corporation's main source of finance

Governmental backing should work in two ways, firstly through major research contracts, and secondly by means of subsidiary capital (a sort of re-insurance) in case of unforeseen difficulties. But the companies should be private, not governmental; and management should not be able to pass on to the government the result of any mistakes. The management of these companies should be judged by the same criteria as any private company management.

One big question remains to be answered: how to gain public confidence and support for a venture of this sort. A good public relations effort would have a strong influence, but it cannot work miracles. We suggested compulsory investment. Let us explain how the 'compulsory' element could come in.

After the tragic November 1966 floods in northern Italy, government circles estimated that the cost of the damage might exceed one quarter of the entire Italian national budget. With the stunning blows to agriculture, transport, commerce and tourism caused by the floods, the prospect was a sharp reduction in national earning power. The government had somehow to raise the money to house the flood-stricken homeless, help the unemployed, and restore roads, ruined farmland and industries. This was a national catastrophe and the Italian Government was justified in taking measures which included new taxation. To raise the urgently needed money the government imposed a 10-lire tax on a litre of petrol.

We believe there is a basic similarity between the Florentine floods and Europe's industrial crisis. It is easier to comprehend the tragic dimensions of the former than the latter, but industrial decay is far more damaging and longer lasting than floods. If urgent compulsory measures were justified for the floods they are justified now for industry.

What about the feasibility, then, of imposing a 10 per cent tax on petrol, against which coupons could be issued? These coupons could be immediately exchangeable for shares of any of the pan-European corporations, at the choice of the owner. He could, if he wished, wait before investing them; he would also be able to invest more than the coupon's face value by paying the difference. This is a bold suggestion to reverse a critical situation, and we offer it as a solution to the problem of applying taxation without alienating public sympathy.

Perhaps the government can invent a better emergency plan. But while European industry continues to be unable to fend for itself, the Americanization of Europe continues.

Chapter Five

DEVELOPING COUNTRIES OF
THE MIDDLE EAST

'Time is as much a resource as money, materials
and men.'
                                        Alfred Sloan

Time is running short for the underdeveloped countries. During our
world-wide research in 1966 we visited twenty-four countries, and
nineteen more countries during 1967. At least three-quarters of
them were countries which could be described as 'less developed'
—industrialized to some degree but insufficiently advanced to compete in world markets. All were hit by the brain drain; in some cases
the loss was as high as eight per cent. The biggest losses naturally
occur in countries which do not have a language barrier with Britain
or America, and many Asian and African countries have English
as an official language. Even in countries which are fiercely proud of
their own traditional language, such as those of the Near East,
English is nevertheless the language of science.

One of the Middle Eastern countries we visited, with a large percentage of students in foreign universities, experiences among those
students a brain drain at the level of between thirty-five and forty
per cent. And, as is usually the case, it is the best of these who
fail to return—the men with technical skills and competence who
can readily find employment in a competitive world.

A high government official in Iran outlined five manpower problems facing his country:

1 Great shortage of skills at all levels, but especially in the top
  jobs
2 Misdirection of the existing potential of qualified experts

3 A lack of proper structure in middle management, and a virtual nonexistence of lower management

4 A brain drain aggravated by the nature of Iranian society and its inertia

5 Brain deterioration because scientists, technologists and executives have little chance to revise their methods, or increase the knowledge gained at university

This situation applies to nearly all Middle East countries and only in degree does it differ from most European ones. Pierre Eddé, president of a leading Beirut bank, described ability as a country's most essential raw material. In assessing a country's stage of development Eddé placed more emphasis on its talent than on its economic resources. So did other Middle Eastern leaders willing and able to see the facts.

Perhaps a minimum standard for a 'developed' country is for at least one per cent of its population to be university graduates. In Lebanon the figure is now approaching one per cent and the government's objective is to exceed it as soon as possible. But we emphasize that this is a minimum requirement and the effectiveness of university education cannot be judged by counting the heads. What happens to the heads afterwards? Today 20,000 trained Lebanese are in São Paulo and 35,000 in Kuwait—enough to seriously disturb Lebanon's development for a generation.

It is also estimated that, out of a total of 700,000 scientists at present working in Britain, America, Canada and Germany, twenty to thirty-five thousand are from India. At the end of 1965 there were 2122 doctors with an Indian qualification employed in Britain. One wonders whether the relative contribution of these M.D.s to the British health services is less than, equal to or greater than the contribution they might have made within the complex of the Indian health service?

A senior government official told of the reasons for brain drain in developing countries which differ from those found in industrialized countries. The illiterate mass has no understanding or appreciation of the efforts of scientists or technologists. High intellectual activity is often considered as a luxury in a country where people do not have enough to eat. The necessary high salaries seem inexcusable. Political agitation does not encourage people to follow any sustained work programme.

The lack of university facilities compels young men to venture abroad for their higher education, and they become exposed to the temptations of life in a sophisticated society before they have learned a sense of responsibility to their own society. Awareness of this problem encourages governments to deny their young men education abroad. And so it goes on, in an ever-tightening circle. A first essential would seem to be a massive education programme at all levels, though many fear this cannot be justified to hungry people or to those who fear the rise of an educated élite in a politically unstable society. As President Johnson once remarked:

'Just as ignorance breeds poverty, poverty breeds ignorance in the next generation.'

The total annual influx of skilled men and women to the United States from underdeveloped and developing nations is less than 10,000, but this figure represents an enormous proportion of the total skill available to these countries. While India and other developing countries realize that they cannot blame Britain and America for having the resources to offer high salaries and large-scale R & D opportunities, they quite naturally object to crucial sectors of their economies being denuded. It seems illogical for America and Britain to pour financial aid into India while, in effect, taking it out again in the form of valuable manpower, wrong not only on ethical grounds but on economic grounds too.

For too long now it has been fashionable to talk of 'assistance' to underdeveloped nations, without considering what form this aid should take. Even before the physical necessities of food and housing, education should be placed first on the list of priorities, the more so because starvation depends as much on the lack of human resources as on lack of food.

The prosperous nations should draw up an imaginative policy which would help poorer countries in both education and finance.[1] The scale of technical aid extended to the developing countries has been constantly increasing, but with the return on investment going the other way. The annual expenditure on foreign skills and training for use of developing countries has already exceeded a figure equivalent to two per cent of the gross national product of these countries, but part of the effort is being dissipated. Over three-fifths of the world's population lives in the developing countries, and by the laws of nature this number will increase with a speed proportionate to their poverty. It looks like a bottomless pit.

The essential task of the day is to advance the brain power of the world. It is quite possible that the newly independent countries have an advantage in their lack of development: they have no massive economic system to reform, no bureaucracy to quietly overthrow. Having nothing, they can only go forward, if they know how to get the mechanism in action. The basic plan to follow could be quite a simple one in concept, though not so simple in execution:

1 Attempt, at a reasonable pace and with a thoroughly worked-out plan, to dampen the population explosion and to develop individual knowledge

2 Make a concentrated effort to improve the people's living and other environmental conditions

3 Widen the educational system, modernize laboratories and curricula

4 Improve the quality of the civil servants by retiring the ageing, and thoroughly retraining the young

5 Provide workable incentives, by placing emphasis on efficiency and performance rather than on years of service, family background, etc.

---

[1] It is disquieting therefore that of America's student population about two per cent (or, more precisely 64,705 in 1962/63) are from overseas compared to Switzerland's twenty-seven per cent; and of that two per cent most are engaged in branches of science which are more important to a highly industrialized nation than to the developing country from which they come.

6 Arrange salary structures so that the highest rewards go to the professionally qualified

7 Work towards a stable political atmosphere to attract foreign investment

8 Set aside three per cent of the gross national product for research—allocating a large proportion to long-term projects

This is the basic path that underdeveloped countries should follow, but it would of course be very naïve to suggest it would be easy. The biggest difficulty would be the lack of education at all levels, for uneducated people do not welcome change. Senior government officials who have been abroad for study or research recognize the need for good management, but their warnings fall largely on deaf ears. 'Underdevelopment is not an economic term—it is a human term,' commented Dr Goodarzi, Minister of State and Secretary General of the High Council of Government Administration of Iran.

A 1966 international education conference, held in Teheran, established that all developing countries are faced with the problem of the brain drain, and, on a country-by-country basis, the characteristics of the problem proved to be surprisingly similar. Many of the students sent abroad for study do not come back and those who do not return are usually the best ones. Those who do come back do not find the proper environment in which to develop. The private sector absorbs the best of the returning graduates, denying government the manpower on which to base its long-term plans. Jealousies arise between departments over those few returning graduates willing to enter government service. Such returning graduates in government service are exposed to the vagaries of periodic political upheaval.

Although the actual number of men involved in an underdeveloped country's brain drain is small, the proportionate loss is very high, and can delay scientific projects for years. It therefore becomes tempting for such countries to institute a 'closed doors' policy—forbidding its graduates to emigrate. But the only country in which we have seen a 'closed doors' policy put into effect so far is Egypt, and it is unlikely to last for long. In man, the desire to make a comfortable living has begun to surpass his desire for isolation, and this will have a significant effect on the evolution towards a mass market for brainpower. In the present day there is little future for an economy which is not mass-oriented.

In Cairo a government organization, Agency for Mobilization and Statistics, has the responsibility of allotting students to their careers. They are assigned to engineering, mathematics, medicine, law and so on and, after graduation, the Agency tells each man where he is going to live and make his career. An engineer may have the rare honour of being left at the university to teach, he may be sent to the Aswan Dam, to the Suez Canal, to an irrigation project in the desert, or to a textile factory. Personal choice counts for little, and the prime consideration is the national necessity as defined by the State Planning Agency.

Every country has to make the best use of its resources so we cannot condemn Egypt out of hand. Men are a major resource in themselves and, used in an able manner, they can be more valuable than oil wells. During a series of lectures we gave a few years ago at the Polish Academy of Sciences, a Polish professor commented that the reason the Russians had advanced so far so fast in two short generations was that they had successfully sacrificed one full generation to meet their objectives. This is how the Russians were able to forge ahead while many of the less committed European nations failed, and it is Russia's example that Egypt has partly adopted.

A government must present its electorate with technological, economic and social justification for such radical changes as are required, and this cannot be done by propounding woolly theories, or even sound theories unless they reach the people's ear. As Dr Goodarzi said: 'For two years in Parliament I tried to convince my colleagues of the wisdom of a rational forward-looking approach. I got an ulcer, but things still stand where they were.' This problem is especially acute in an ill-educated society and a wide-ranging and forceful public relations and advertising campaign must be brought into operation, one specially adapted to the needs of a largely illiterate public.

One of the Ministers we met identified three types of opponents to change. Firstly, the 'empire' defenders who quite simply refuse to accept economic reform as a reality; secondly, those who do not understand the need for change; and thirdly, those who are quite simply afraid of change. Another senior government official remarked: 'During a parliamentary debate on a new law for the promotion of civil servants, one of the ageing deputies rose up in the ranks of the opposition to remark: "I was chief of personnel thirty years ago and we did it the old traditional way. This is still the best way." Well, what can you answer to that?'

It is virtually impossible to convince static nations of the need for long-term industrial planning without quoting purely local examples. Perhaps we are asking too much of them at present. But these nations, should they fail to realize in the near future the need for economic and social revolution, will never be able to compete in the world market, and that would be dangerous not only economically but politically. It is our intention to show that the two interests are one.

Few people would consider Israel as among the 'underdeveloped' nations, but there are aspects of her economic condition which hold her back more severely than many poorer countries. Perhaps the most serious of these is a very high proportion of well-educated people in an underpopulated country whose higher education races ahead of its industries' capacity to absorb it, leading to a brain drain of alarming proportions.

Despite all the evidence of a growing material prosperity, the brain drain inhibits the nation from moving towards the sort of future envisaged by government and university. The men whom we met during our visit forecast that in ten years their country would boast a completely modern technology based on advanced cybernetics. This they see within the framework of a policy which treats talent as an enormous capital investment. But will the brain drain permit a realization of Israel's plans?

Official sources estimate that between 4000 and 5000 Israelis with academic training are working abroad. In terms of ratio this is equivalent to about 450,000 American graduates choosing to follow their career overseas. In practically all cases, limited career opportunity is the cause of the migration.

Alexander Goldberg, President of the Technion, estimates that most of the 300 graduates from his school now working in the United States are electronic engineers. The main reason, he believes, is that forty-six per cent of faculty graduates had found employment in Israel as technicians rather than as designers and engineers. This disparity between professional training and professional opportunity is mainly attributed to a lack of co-ordination between the development of Israel's industry and her institutions of higher education.

The solution to the brain drain should be based on the progressive development of industry within the scope of its university output. Informed people with whom we discussed the brain drain were of the opinion that Israel should follow an orderly stepwise course in developing her resources of ability, based on one of the most promising industries: advanced information systems. Such an industry could offer the challenging employment required by those of her people highly trained in the modern disciplines.

But Israel does not have the internal market to sustain an advanced information systems effort for long, and unless it is successful in finding foreign markets (in an enormously competitive field) the industry will grow top-heavy, leading to a further aggravation of the brain drain.

It has been suggested, for example, that the Israeli information systems industry should be operated through a system of multinational companies. This would permit manufacturing centres not only for international markets, but also for world-wide national markets with specific needs. Such decentralized economic and industrial administration may indeed be the best hope for all nations which do not have the necessary mass population at home to sustain a constant expansion of industry.

Unfortunately Israel has a political problem which is not merely confined to its own relations with its Arab neighbours. Many highly industrialized countries are nervous of offending the Arab world by dealing with Israel. Enlightened Israelis are trying to demonstrate to the Arabs (with little success so far) that a multinational company centred in Israel could be as beneficial to the Arabs as to the Israelis themselves. It is the same story as in Europe. Countries must forget their national feelings and pool their economic resources if they are to compete with the technological giants.

Had it not been for this drawback, we consider this world-wide approach as the best twentieth-century idea for a 'decentralized economic and industrial administration'. It is a sound hope for all nations where the mass effect cannot be internally brought to bear.

In Israel, nevertheless, some people are sceptical as to how this strategy is going to succeed. Their concern mostly stems from the fact that the brain drain Israel currently suffers will see to it that the proper resources will never accumulate for an ambitious plan. And they are afraid that nothing short of a total attack along the line of our discussion will be able to attract a very high calibre of recruit.

That last reference is not just a concern of yesterday. It dates several years back and its essence is best exemplified by a question posed in the mid-fifties, by the Israeli Government, regarding the evolution of grey matter. Norbert Weiner answered: 'Send your people to M.I.T. and we will think out loud together.' The thinking aloud took place and led to the following conclusions:

1 The scope of the evolution of grey matter must be planned ahead. The time ranges for grey matter development are more critical than for, say, the evolution of new products and systems

2 In Israel, the relative mass of grey matter is on the decrease. Contributing to this is not only the brain drain but also the

substantial migration from countries with a lower level of development

3 Intensive educational programmes both enhance the level of cultural development of a country, and help in the effective integration of different populations, customs and ethics

PART II

THE KNOWLEDGE REVOLUTION IN ACTION

Chapter Six

NEW CHALLENGES FOR MANAGEMENT

'The requirements of our science and technological based industries are outstripping our
capacity to produce them.'   John F. Kennedy

Success and expansion in industry are dependent on awareness of
the need for change and on the ability of management to identify
themselves with it. Weakness lies in the incapacity to carry the
change to its logical conclusion of profit and growth. It has always
been so.

Pliny the Elder tells of the glassmaker who invented a marvellous
flexible glass and rushed it to his ruler with expectations of a great
reward. But the Emperor Tiberius promptly ordered the glassmaker's factory to be destroyed for fear that the new material would
devalue the emperor's storehouse of silver and gold. Governments,
until recently, did worse than destroy factories and laboratories
working on R & D—they were indifferent to them. Now they have
learned to encourage R & D but not often in the proper spirit.

To face the challenge of the next thirty years, nations, industries
and men must look to year 2000, make plans for technology and
science and its advances and foresee what the estimated seven billion people who will be living by that time may demand. Will the
underdeveloped nations remain largely agrarian economies with
low living standards because of lack of leadership, resources, capital
and knowhow? Will the intermediate developed nations still lag
behind the world leaders? How will these developments affect industrial demand? Energy consumption? [1] Educational needs?

[1] For energy consumption the forecast, for instance, is that it will grow more
rapidly than population and will therefore require a major expansion of coal,
petroleum, water and nuclear power capacity on a world-wide basis.

The research in depth done by the Engineering Advisory Council identifies in a masterly manner the highlights of year 2000:[1]

1. The United States will be a resource-poor nation, so a greater proportion of effort must be channelled to exploitation of remaining resources and to the development of substitutes

2. America will be devoting considerable energy to solutions of large-scale systems problems of water supply, transportation, urban development and re-development, and communication

3. By 2000, nearly half the United States population between the ages of twenty and sixty may be college graduates. A similar but smaller increase will occur in Russia and the major European countries. Thus, the leading industrial countries will continue to expand their intellectual skills at a rapid rate.

4. California will lead America in the development of complex systems and will make additional contributions to the know-how underlying production of capital goods consumed within and exported from the United States. California's natural resources will be relatively more depleted than those of the United States as a whole

5. California, with a far greater investment in education than the rest of the United States and more limited natural resources, will lead in the export of knowhow

6. America's comparative economic advantage in world trade will be knowhow. Since knowhow will be their export product, they will have learned how to measure their investment in knowhow and to exploit its use profitably. It will be represented in their engineering as well as in their organizational and financial skill.

This study and its projections were made in an effort to visualize the years up to 2000, in order to help define a university curriculum able to produce engineers and scientists capable of facing the chal-

[1] 'An Engineering Master Plan Study for the University of California', September 1965.

lenges of that time. How many European nations (or universities) have done something comparable? Not surprisingly the research has revealed new insights into the role of the engineer in our future society. It indicates that nearly everything related to man will continue to grow, in some cases exponentially: population, knowledge, productivity, consumption, the living standard and, hopefully, the quality of man himself.

As a result of this growth, man's resources of energy, materials, information, land, water and air, will be used in ever greater and more complex ways. To avoid depletion, men, industries and nations will have to devise better, more efficient methods. This means that science must continue to make discoveries to ease the problem of exploitation, just as science over the last 100 years has made discoveries which demand exploitation and lead to expanding consumption.

That is why research and the future of nations are so much linked together. That is also why research and education have synthesized a mass effect which has brought the Knowledge Revolution into being. The challenge of growth brought about by the Knowledge Revolution calls for an increased emphasis on the systems aspect, relating the contributions of specialists to one another and to the human needs which are being met. Systems studies will make an impact in urban planning, transportation, space, communications, information storage and retrieval, and resource management. Much can be said about this last subject.

We are just leaving an era of resource protection, and entering the era of resource management. Around 1940 it became generally apparent that the natural resources were limited, that the increasing burden of discharged wastes on the water and air resources was presenting a real threat to their continued utilization, and that the land itself could be damaged by the kind of development which took place on it. We therefore entered the period of resource protection. This period coincided at the outset with the explosive growth of industries and urban areas during the years of World War II.

Yet of late it has become tragically apparent that our society has

77

never established any standards of resources consumption or of environmental quality. In fact it did not have even a goal concerning the utilization of its resources. This cannot continue. It is quite evident that the simple principles of resource protection will not enable us to meet the resource needs of the last third of this century. Social strife will result just from that. As the population continues to grow, it will soon outstrip the available sources of air, water, minerals, energy and land, unless the concept of resource management is put into practice.

The management of the resources of energy and material must be geared to meet the needs of the world-wide explosion of knowledge and population and of the pressure for parity from different levels of society and from different nations. The social upheaval which brought the French economy to a standstill in May 1968 is a case in point. Lack of planning leads to disaster. The possibility and implications of social strife make regional and worldwide forward planning in the fields of systems and resources mandatory. The Engineering Master Plan Study identified the following as the key issues in the years ahead.

1 Employment of the unskilled will be a major problem in the West. The evolution towards a technologically complex capital-goods economy will lead to more automation and less demand for unskilled labour

2 There will be a limited number of people with technological 'knowhow' throughout most of the world. The concentrated sources of knowledge will be the United States, Western Europe, the Soviet Union, Japan and China

3 Much of the world will continue to lack the social, political, and economic stability of the United States, Russia and Europe. Therefore, worldwide educational development, knowledge and intellectual skills will remain relatively low·

4 Most countries of Asia, Africa, and Latin America will continue to be industrially underdeveloped compared to the West,

Russia, Japan and China. Japan's industrial and technological capacities will improve at a rate comparable to that of the West; and she will be a major exporter of consumer and capital goods. China may emerge by 2000 A.D. as a leading industrial nation, but with a largely self-contained economy

5 Large segments of the world's population will still live in relative poverty. Undernourishment, unemployment, poor housing, little educational development, and meagre medical care will remain prevalent throughout much of Asia, Africa, and Latin America.

The dual challenge of the Knowledge Revolution and of Resource Management calls for an increased emphasis on developing new sources and new methods. A great deal of acumen will be required to find means to apply new scientific discoveries for man's benefit as soon as possible. The challenge of the knowledge industry demands, as a prerequisite, life-long learning, updating and upgrading. The ASEE Goals of Engineering Education Study [1] has classified continuing education needs as follows:

1 UPGRADING a person's education (a person may work towards a graduate degree to raise the level of his formal capabilities)

2 UPDATING a person's education (a person who received a B.Sc. degree ten years ago may wish to take course work to make his formal education comparable to that of a person receiving a B.Sc. degree this year)

3 DIVERSIFICATION into new fields (a person educated in one field may seek to obtain some formal education in another field, but not necessarily at a higher degree level)

4 MATURING of a person's education (a person may add a new perspective in his existing field, such as the inclusion of

[1] Goals of Engineering Education Study, Information Document No. 4 (Initial Report to the Institutional Committees concerning Graduate Education in Engineering), American Society for Engineering Education, May 1964.

financial, temporal, political, and social factors, but again without raising the academic level of his education).

The aura that enshrouds most European top level management (and governmental authorities) gives no assurance that these needs will be met. Ability is revealed in acts. Are decisions responsible or irresponsible? Are facts carefully analysed? Are the consequences of, say, abandoning large-scale research projects fully evaluated? Are not merely the immediate consequences considered, but the long term consequences as well—of which the brain drain may be a major one?

One crucial task is to find managers who can direct a scientist's work towards the economy's most vital needs. Industry today has to handle explosive problems of growth which are quite without precedent. The urgent demands of overworked staffs, insufficient funds for research and development, rapid product obsolescence and fierce competition in the marketplace, hamper both the industrial management and the governmental executives responsible for the financial and industrial health of the nation. The essence of the Knowledge Revolution is that the solution of these problems now and in the future depends entirely on the sophisticated use of brainpower. Brains are the modern capital. This makes our most urgent task the proper planning of education, personal development, and the utilization of talent.

THE POWER OF PLANNING

The beginning of European failure dates back to years of neglect in R & D. The present resistance to large-scale 'change' can be related to this neglect covering the whole spectrum of activity from industrial operations to the university system. Europe is suffering from a creeping, but not incurable, malaise. Strong medicine will be needed to remedy our morale, government, labour relations, universities and, above all, our vision of the future. It must begin with planning—and planning must begin with management.

Europeans are understandably frustrated for they earnestly

believe their intellect and sensibility should make them world leaders. But they forget that somehow, possibly through complacency and self-deception, they have lost the power to lead. Europe has contained first-class powers for centuries, but she came out of the last war with no apparent desire to keep the initiative. Self-congratulation about radar, penicillin, or hovercraft, is no substitute for effective leadership. Invention without exploitation is useless. As Anthony Wedgwood Benn remarked: 'You can't eat Nobel prizes.'

Views symptomatic of a national obsession can be dangerous. European governments (and managements) have too often been prey to the Big Bang theory of the economic, scientific and industrial universe. The theory that one large decision in itself solves all the problems in that area is fallacious.

The ills besetting European industry are far more radical than any brave speeches can cure. In almost any western European country there are hosts of middle-sized, family-owned businesses, whose intentions are not to grow but to continue to supply a comfortable income for their owners. There would seem to be something general in the European business mentality that inhibits an output-minded, consumer-oriented attitude. Some say that this phenomenon is the by-product of a high level of civilization—but high levels of civilization cannot be maintained without the underpinning of expansive economic prosperity.

Even world-renowned manufacturers still avoid gambling in the science-intensive mass market. The firm with no stockpile is certainly 'conservative'. Production schedules are based on the number of goods ordered. You don't decide to buy 'this' or 'that' product—you order one, and may wait for months while a competitor's model (probably from the multi-national company) is easily available. This may help cut down the operating expenses, but it is hardly a policy of planning for aggressive growth, and aggressive growth is the mainspring of tomorrow's industry.

The technological gap between the countries which are moving ahead and those still reluctant to enter into the great scientific technological arena is widening. So great is the impact of the gap that even governments who over the last ten years have tried to bridge it with short-term measures are no longer certain of their effectiveness.

We are not, however, praying for a technological miracle, but are warning even the most short-sighted statesmen and industrialists of the consequences if they are not prepared to plan, and to pay for, large-scale change. Yet it is more discouraging to realize that we have no assurance that Western Europe really understands the risk it is running with respect to its future. Is this due to a failure in forecasting, a lack of willingness to go ahead with a determined plan, a reluctance to pay the price of change, or perhaps all three?

Management (at both company and government levels) must face the realities of industrial evolution. Smallness must not be used as an excuse for timidity, for cancelling or impeding essential research programmes, or for stopping altogether, or for never starting in the first place. But small size is a fact; a fact which deprives many companies (and nations) of the 'cumulative advantages' resulting from mass research, mass manufacturing and mass marketing. The colossal resources at the disposal of the United States offer to the American companies the possibility of increasing the gap between themselves and any competition from Western Europe.

It would be completely illogical to regard the large American company as a dragon which must be slain or at least brought to heel. And it would be equally irrational to disregard or fail to appreciate the great advantages to be derived from business mergers and diversification. The unimaginative, inhibited attitude to these subjects has put the small, European company at a tremendous disadvantage at a time when science-based industries require increasingly greater resources.

Precious time has been lost. At present the mass technology and mass marketing era is still, relatively speaking, in its infancy, and we have barely begun to feel the impact. But the action is developing much faster than many leaders of today realize. Europe must move fast in unison with the technological giants if she does not wish to be left out of the race.

THE MANAGEMENT OF CHANGE

In the years ahead it will be a fatal mistake to underestimate the impact of human resources. As we have already stated, human resources are the crucial factor behind scientific and technological advancement. It is no good having mineral resources without the knowledge of mining and manufacture, which is why Europe has led the world for so long in spite of the wealth lying a few feet below the ground in Africa, Asia and Australia. Highly talented nations tend to invent or discover new resources to keep them always at the front of progress. And, in an increasingly better-educated world, Europe must retain that position, for she has limited natural resources to shore her economy against the advancing tide.

This necessitates an acceptance of new values and policies and a rejection of attitudes which obstruct progress. A director of a leading British company commented during our discussion that profits in Europe have been a dirty word since the end of World War II. A complete generation was brought up with the illogical conviction in its mind that the only useful function of profit was to demonstrate how antisocial management really is.

Two broad movements swept through Europe at the end of World War II, which took a firm stand against profits. Both movements pressed hard for ill-defined ideals of social justice through human equality which promised to be difficult to identify and to implement. The socialists did their best to set up the Welfare State. Not to be outdone, the Catholics set up the anti-profit theme as one of their ideals. Unfortunately both politicians and electorate were convinced by their arguments, and profit-making became slightly unclean.

Enlightened industrialists and national leaders of this period who saw the absurdity of these views of profit-making were afraid to speak their minds for fear of being labelled fascists. Even more serious was the indoctrination of junior executives during the late

1940s with the same anti-profit ideas. This in itself was a danger signal, but was ignored. It resulted in misguided investment and industrial policies of whole nations for many years. It is today that the results are being felt; and it is today that this attitude must be changed. Happily, even the trades unions, who fought tooth and nail against profits, seem to be waking up to the harm which has been done.

Like a company planning its new products, government needs able management to plan the future of its industries and people. National development thus depends on wide-thinking systems management. No government can afford to perpetuate the forms of 'prehistoric' thinking so familiar in the past; it cannot afford to fight the problems of the seventies with the attitudes of the fifties. Establishing the most dynamic method of economic and industrial expansion should be the main goal of European governmental and management planning. The first priority is investment in R & D, the development of ability and the institution of realistic forms of incentive. Unlike previous measures of government and industry, this should be a comprehensive and sustained drive. It involves selecting priorities for growing industries, while at the same time increasing the rewards for enterprising management.

'Britain is Best' is no longer a slogan to fall back on but a state to aspire to. If governments merely continue to talk about the merits of our traditional 'home-grown' industry and to extol the virtues of the nation's window display, then the technological, industrial and cultural future of Western Europe may well be beyond redemption.

As we strive to manage the necessary changes in our economic way of life, our manifesto ought to be:

'Long-term plans backed up with much courage will be necessary to build a scientific and industrial structure able to withstand the challenges of the future.

'Investments in human capital are vital for productivity, indeed for survival. Nothing can stop an organization which continues to pay full attention to the acquisition, development and utilization of talent.'

A researcher in the humanities has summed up in the following manner the history of ancient Athens and the Athenians: his words could well apply to Europe in twenty years time, if we do not take their warning seriously:

'In the last analysis, they wanted freedom, security, and a comfortable life—and they lost them all: security, comfort and freedom. The more the Athenians wanted to give nothing to society and to receive everything in exchange, the more they were overtaken by evolution. When the freedom to which they were aspiring had become nothing more than freedom from responsibility, then Athens ceased being free and has never been free since.'

Chapter Seven

THE KNOWLEDGE INDUSTRY

'Brains are like hearts—they go where they are
appreciated.'   Robert McNamara

For nearly two centuries the Industrial Revolution has been the
dominant economic force in the world. Few people yet realize that
the Industrial Revolution is now dead and has been superseded by
another: the Knowledge Revolution. This new revolution is
characterized by an almost unlimited world-wide demand for brains
and talent.

The Knowledge Revolution implies, for companies and nations
alike, a gigantic cost. It requires clear thinking. It calls for far-out
perspectives. That is why managers of a former generation are out
of touch with the economics of the present. America spends a
quarter of its gross national product on the production and distribution of all kinds of knowledge—from the most important to the
most trivial. Included in this sum are $60 billion for education,
$27 billion for research and development, $50 billion for all communications media, $15 billion for information machines and $30
billion for information services.

Apart from this expenditure it has been calculated that spending
on the 'intangible' commodities of advanced research and knowledge is growing 2·4 times as fast as spending on physical goods and
other services. 'Spending on intangibles' may seem a peculiar part
of progress, but the very idea of a 'knowledge industry' revolu-
tionizes both traditional ways of thinking and current practices.

Let us start with the fundamentals. There exists in the world
today a grossly uneven geographic distribution of top scientific personnel. As we stated in Part I, while no country has a monopoly on

the production of scientists, a few fortunate countries are the dominant employers and consequently gain a disproportionate economic advantage.

In a well-ordered transitional atmosphere two countries, Russia and the United States, are moving from a society based on natural resources to one based on human resources. The picture of a society centred on human resources is fully supported by present experience. Industry is increasingly placing a premium on mental alertness and concentration, and man is paid for his brain power rather than for his physical strength. Education and industry, until now two distinct entities, have started inter-weaving with one another.

How did this whole process get started? With the huge rise in world demand for goods in the immediate post-war years, American industry went into a massive boom which has set the pattern for her economic success ever since. This industrial thrust was both preceded and accompanied by a boom in university education.

The huge internal investment of the war years, and the great concentration of effort on capital goods industries, have been directed towards meeting the sudden surge of enormously profitable sales in world markets. The industrial structure thus established has been the mainspring of the American economic expansion which has continued ever since. On the knowledge side, the strong contributing factor was the historical accident of the 'G.I. Bill'.

Originally conceived as a means to ease the unemployment problem at the end of the War, the G.I. Bill became the fount of higher education. A colossal (for its time) number of G.I.s poured into American universities on government scholarships, thus changing mass unemployment into a glut of qualified men, who became the nucleus of the Knowledge Revolution. Britain, too, made vast investments during the war years to sustain an admirable defensive and then an offensive effort. When the War ended British industry accounted for some 20 per cent of world trade.[1] But in terms of share in brain power, nothing spectacular can be recorded.

[1] Since then her share has dropped to half as much.

87

The goldmine that Americans have shown themselves to possess is an understanding of the new economic conditions, especially of their dependence on education. This is demonstrated by the newly evolved relationship between industry and university. In years past, in America as in Europe today, university life enjoyed a glamorous detachment from the vulgar commercial world. To become more than superficially educated men had to abandon the ordinary life of their times and live for many years a cloistered existence in ill-equipped laboratories. It was a mentally stimulating activity, but not a financially rewarding one, and the university faculty could truly be said to work for love.

It would seem that Europe still encourages this sort of situation. But in America now the pursuit of learning does not necessitate a complete withdrawal from industrial life, even if it entails, as it often may, some fifteen years at the university. With an ever-increasing dependency on highly educated talent, American industry has stimulated the universities to produce the skills it requires, and a close relationship has grown up with a consequent interchange of ideas. Universities have become an industry; and industry has become a kind of university. This is explored further in Chapter Eight.

Under the impact of advanced technology in Europe, America and Russia, an estimated 150 million jobs will change their character over the next thirty-five years. Children now starting school may find it necessary to change vocations at least three times during their lifetime. To survive, they will have to be versatile to an extent unknown in the past. The same applies to industries and universities. The changing face of both industry and education over the last ten years is only an indication of what is to come. As the economies of industrialized nations shift from being production-oriented to being ideas-oriented, industry and education must plan together to produce that raw material which a combined Europe has more of than any civilization in the world: Brains.

Table VI shows the density of university-level training in the world's leading technological countries. We have compiled these data on the basis of our personal research—all information being officially submitted to us by universities and by embassies.

TABLE VI

University Level Training for the 'Knowledge Revolution'

COUNTRY	Enrolled students 1962	Estimated 4-year percentage increase in enrolment 1962-6	Enrolled students 1966	Enrolment percentage of age group 20–4 years	20–4-year-olds as percentage of population
United States	3,200,000	72%	5,526,000[1]	43%	6·5%
Russia	2,400,000	67%	4,000,000 est.	24%	7·5% est.
Canada	130,000	77%	205,000	20·5%	6·8%
France	250,000	100%	500,000	16%	6·5% est.
Japan	760,000	80%	1,370,000 est.	13·2%	9·5%
Sweden	30,000	107%	62,000	11%	6·5% est.
Belgium	30,000	80%	54,000	10%	6·8%
Germany	220,000	27%	280,000[1]	7·5%	6·5% est.
Italy	220,000	30%	284,000	6·9%	7·8%
England	140,000	18%	165·000	4·8%	6·8%
Switzerland	20,000	50%	30,000[1]	4·8%	—
India	—	—	1,700,000	3·8%	9·0%

[1] Foreign Students are 2% in the US; 8% in Germany; 27·5% in Switzerland

It is hardly surprising that responsible men in Europe are growing increasingly worried at the widening technological gap between themselves and the United States. But because the universities and research laboratories are the power that has created this gap, the development of a policy for science must of necessity centre around the knowledge industry as such. Britain devotes more of her national budget to research and development than any single country in Europe, spending more than Germany, Italy and the three Benelux countries put together, but she continues to fall rapidly behind America and Russia. Europe's only hope is to combine its resources.

As with all evolution, the American knowledge revolution proves to be irreversible. For many years, economists had been puzzling over the fact that traditional concepts of capital investment had failed to explain adequately the growth of a dynamic economy. Only recently have the economists turned to studies of the human intellect and to their potential profitability.

Leading industrial analysts and economic planners contend that in the years ahead the contribution of education to economic growth will exceed that of physical capital. And they say that the 'return on invested capital' in science and formal knowledge will probably account for more than one-fifth of a nation's growth. They are probably right, for the contribution of the knowledge revolution to economic growth has, so far, more than measured up to expectations. Knowledge has become a major national resource as important to a country as its land and mineral wealth. Advanced technology in the future will decide not only the rise and fall of companies, professions and social classes—it will decide the future of nations.

But knowledge by itself is not enough—there must be the management which knows how to put that knowledge to work. It was a characteristic of the Industrial Revolution that nations kept an anxious eye on the flow of goods and raw materials, and maintained accurate accounts of their balances of trade. It is a symptom of the Knowledge Revolution that nations are becoming equally sensitive to the 'balance of ability'.

Alexandria was the first state to enjoy an organized brain gain. With America, the lure is the accumulation and development of scientific knowledge. In Alexandria it was Ptolemy's library. This storehouse of knowledge was conceived on a tremendous scale, and historians say that whenever a stranger brought an unknown book to Egypt, he had to have it copied for the library. For the purpose of dissemination, a considerable staff of copyists was engaged continually in making duplicates of all the more popular and necessary works, and in time Alexandria's Library became a book-selling business.

Callimachus, the head of the Library during the time of Ptolemy II and III, saw to the systematic arrangement and cataloguing of the voluminous accumulation of knowledge and it attracted scholars from all over the known world (though mostly from Athens). Ptolemy II ingeniously offered these learned men twice the salary earned in their country of origin to stay and work in Alexandria, and Alexandria's heyday had begun. Today's situation contains striking parallels, and for a country which suffers from the brain drain, the future does not look rosy. The responsibility lies with those reactionaries in the 'drain' countries who cannot or will not adapt as society requires. The problem is that the knowledge revolution has introduced change with such bewildering speed that the average human being cannot adapt to it. When a man is uncertain of his direction he stands still.

History repeats itself. As was the case with the decaying world of ancient Greece, in the second half of the twentieth century countries which educate more talent than they employ suffer a 'brain drain'. It follows that the correctly oriented industrial countries tend to enjoy an accelerating increase of talent as young brains are lured to the centre of present-day knowledge, as they were to Ptolemy's Alexandria.

European management (industrial and governmental) will be judged by the way in which it appreciates that the time for bold, imaginative approaches to R & D is *now*, rather than five years hence, or even next year. European leaders must remember that through their own efforts they have at least started to push the number of university students up by about 20 per cent per year. This is indeed commendable—but the task does not end there; this is only the beginning.

In Europe today, the number of postgraduate students studying for research degrees is far from impressive. We hope and presume that this number will rise as universities and colleges expand. But at the same time the sophistication, complexity and cost of modern scientific equipment rises by another 5 per cent each year. Taken together, the growth and cost figures are a sound foundation on which to base an evaluation of the investments required for a given expansion. The situation calls for immediate action, but Europe may well wonder how industry, which seems unable to command respect in the leadership of research and development, will manage the new international industrial colossus.

For twenty years everything from product innovation to industrial research in Europe has got behind schedule, and now technology is well below the level that can support a healthy and growing economy. R & D projects and similar undertakings certainly cost big money, but is the brain drain supposed to be of no cost or consequence? A rough estimate, based on some fifteen years of study and related experience, indicates that in America each 'ready brain' lost by a country represents a minimum identifiable loss of $50,000 a year to its economy. It may be a great deal more.

Britain has good reasons for being deeply concerned. She is losing senior university professors, and an estimated 18 per cent of her total output of Ph.D. graduates a year to research jobs abroad. If this loss of talent continues it will slow the nation's technological advance and it will shake its social, economic and political foundations. Other European countries, Germany for example, face the same challenge. But they, too, appear to have failed in making an honest effort to keep the best of their men at home.

Top men are too often left with minor jobs, from which they emigrate to greener fields. The outcome is that second-level jobs are accepted only by the second-rate. Drain countries will have to be content with these people because of their own failure to offer the opportunities that an intelligent and educated man desires.

It is not yet realized by many governments and managements that the accomplished scientist, engineer or economist needs far more than sympathy or even acceptance. Seen as a packaged product, the university graduate is undoubtedly more marketable than any other product that can be made by human ingenuity, and this should be freely acknowledged.

Scientists and technologists cannot be condemned to clerking functions by the uneducated few of a country's current élite. They know that they can find opportunities in any advanced environment they wish to choose. To an increasing degree, today's innovator is a scientist with fifteen years or more of formal education leading to the award of a doctorate. Gaining or losing the brain power of men like him may well mean the difference between growth and stagnation for a whole economy.

THE PRICE OF PROGRESS

Many countries do not yet realize that their true wealth is in the minds of men, and that a net outflow of scientific talent puts them in danger of being unable to compete in the new world.

The situation of most countries is serious enough, but for some of them the position is aggravated by apparent ignorance of the dangers. When Admiral Rickover gave a lecture at the Propeller Club in Athens and suggested the country should do something to develop and keep its Ph.D.s, he took his listeners by surprise. They were not sure who these exotic-sounding 'Ph.D.s' were. Rickover gave an evaluation which merits close attention:

'In respect to what he can contribute in technological and industrial progress, one Ph.D. is worth twenty graduate engineers. Only the countries which can maintain a fair-sized Ph.D. force can hope to participate in the progress of the future.'

Some nations are lucky enough to have enlightened rulers who can lead them successfully into the Knowledge Revolution. At a meeting in June 1966, Amir-Abbas Hoveyda, the Prime Minister of Iran, told us: 'Development is in the human brain. Under-development is also in the human brain. And this is almost independent of economic and social conditions.' But not all political leaders have so much grasp of fundamental economic truths.

Europe cannot defy or ignore the knowledge revolution. She can only join it, or suffer a brain drain as yet unparalleled and resign herself to a second-class position among the world's continents. It will certainly be impossible for one European country to face the challenge of the Knowledge Revolution alone. We referred to this in Chapter Four when we suggested the urgent need for pan-European enterprises and a method of effective Europe-wide financing.

A country's research budget must be planned years in advance, but one difficulty is that the continuation of the brain drain may completely alter the estimated picture of the future. Sir Harrie Massey's Council for Scientific Policy has warned that a continuation of the present growth rate of expenditure on scientific research and development will soon be too much for the British economy to bear. The Council forecast that if expenditure continues to increase at its present rate, it will have risen eightfold by 1984.

This warning, accurate within its own limited context, misses the real point. Well before 1984, the leading industrial nations of the world will be those who have spent enough on R & D to be a magnet for ability, retaining their own talent and perhaps attracting more talent from elsewhere. The 'return' on R & D expenditure, as we have already seen, can be the best investment governments can make. But is anybody listening?

During the 1960s the United States has spent about ten times more *per capita* on research and some four times as much altogether as Europe. In 1966 alone, the American government poured $16 billion into research and development efforts most of which went into defence, aerospace, aircraft and electronics. These are the areas in which American firms are learning to master staggering complexities on technology's frontiers, not only applying their knowledge in the conquering of world markets, but acting as a magnet to scientists from the rest of the world.

With their vast capital and huge market, American companies risk fortunes beyond Europe's vision. In one year General Electric gambled a sum rumoured to be $60 million in nuclear power production, but it now has a backlog of orders of $2 billion in that field. RCA gambled $130 million on colour television before showing any profits. And let nobody believe that American companies are unique in displaying this forward thrust. The challenge comes not from Europe but from Japan—and Europe may pay the final bill of the Japanese thrust as, in years past, she paid that of the American.

If the last twenty years have been those of the American challenge in Europe, the coming twenty years promise to be the years of the Japanese challenge. Shipbuilding, in tonnage, is one long-standing specific example. The manufacturing of micro-computers is another example—and a much more recent one. Thirty-five firms around the world have thrust into this field. Of these fifteen are European, eight are American and twelve are Japanese. But if integrated circuits are taken as a typical example, no European firm is involved, while four American and nine Japanese firms are the forerunners. The Japanese outpace the Americans by more than two to one.

Such references dramatize the European failure to get results. At present, Britain spends on scientific research something approaching £1,000 million. But the feeling of achievement is not there. Yet, if the expenditure so far has failed to stop the brain drain, it would seem foolish to consider levelling it off. It is rather like trying to do without oxygen. Rather Britain should increase its expenditure while also improving the management and exploitation of the R & D effort.

To some degree greater efficiency could be achieved by re-deploying money being already committed to lesser value tasks. The Council for Scientific Policy hopes to encourage a greater flexibility with funds and man-power so that new projects are not restricted by older ones which absorb the available funds. But this is still only picking at the problem. The assessment of a research programme's merits depends on its potential benefits not only to pure science but also to industry and to education, and the budget should be planned with these factors in mind.

Rethinking, based on a target of increased cost/effectiveness, would involve the closer liaison between research councils, universities, governments and industries which Europe badly lacks. The creeping fear of European businessmen is that they are condemned by their governments' lack of planning to fall continuously behind their American counterparts in the crucial technological race. There are several reasons for this, and an obvious one is the failure to move from the research laboratory to the production bench to the international market. We discuss this more fully in the last chapter.

The lead of American research and development is demonstrated effectively in what we call the 'technological balance of payments'. This compares the amount the United States earns from its licences and patents with the amount it spends on acquiring foreign knowledge. The balance is strongly in favour of the American companies. In the early 1960s Western Europe (Britain, France, West Germany, Holland and Belgium) paid some $250 million per year for American knowhow and sold in exchange $45 million worth. This balance was nearly double the $111 million paid by Europe to the US in the late 1950s, and the discrepancy is bound to increase.

We have an absolutely unique opportunity at this period of our history to plan the future instead of merely letting it happen. For more than a century the industrialized countries have been plagued by the problems created by the transition from a mostly agrarian to an urban and suburban society. Rural markets have declined; city suburbs have grown too fast; congestion and decay have overtaken the nation's cities. As a result, housing is inadequate, and slums proliferate. Local and national transportation is badly overtaxed. Recreation areas practically vanish. Air and water pollution increases. Municipal costs continue to soar. And so on. No one could have foreseen these results of the Industrial Revolution. But today we do have not only the knowledge to assess the future but the power to shape it according to our desires. We must exercise that power and not begrudge the cost.

Chapter Eight

THE EDUCATIONAL 'RESIDUAL'
AND THE BRAIN FACTORIES

'The future has always been the province of
those who planned for it.'   Tex Thornton

The analysis of statistical data on industrial development has led
Odd Aukrust, of the Central Bureau of Statistics, Oslo, to talk of
the 'educational residual'. If the current rate of growth in the most
advanced economies were permanently maintained for five decades,
the industrial investment rate would apparently lead to a far smaller
expansion of the gross national product than the thirty-sevenfold
growth estimated. The output growth rates the world has experienced during the fifties and the sixties are, by all historical
standards, extremely high.

To make his point, Aukrust starts with the statistical observation
that there are by now about twenty countries in the world which
have statistics on national income and national product that cover
fifty years or more. In only one of these countries has the long-term
per capita (real) growth rate averaged over 2·5 per cent a year.
Rates of rather less than an average 1·5 per cent a year have been
much more typical. But in the post-war period some countries have
been able to grow at such extremely high rates as 5 per cent or
more. How do we account for this phenomenon?

Economists tend to accept as an established fact that the observed
differences in the growth rates of America and of the European
countries are real differences. They cannot be explained away by
differing statistical methods or by differences in industrial structure,
for these vary little from one European country to another. Some
countries have devoted more resources to capital formation than

others, but there seems to be only a tenuous connection between the accumulation of capital and the growth of output; more capital can no longer be considered the all-important factor of national growth.

The statistical evidence of Aukrust (Table VII) indicates that over long periods the differences in countries' growth rates tend to even out. It would seem that, over a span of thirty years, growth trends are determined by forces other than those which create short-term fluctuations (e.g. a country catching up on a wartime setback). Temporary set-backs are made good and evened out, more or less automatically, by means of some important underlying residual factor of growth.

This gives a new dimension to the knowledge industry, and to the Knowledge Revolution. In the long term it is the 'human capital', the ability of man to devise new technological possibilities, his gradually increasing insight and cleverness, which determine the speed of progress, and this happens almost irrespective of the rate of capital accumulation. Aukrust concludes:

'We have sufficient evidence today . . . that there are important factors of growth—besides labour and capital—hiding behind the residual (growth) factors. We have referred to them in a loose way as "technical progress", "organization". But what are these factors?

'The only honest answer to this is, I believe, that we do not really know. I am tempted to go further: we may never know for sure. For how can we ever hope to determine the relative importance of the many factors which determine productivity, ranging from a government's economic policy to the competitive spirit of entrepreneurship?

'Still, behind most of the factors which we could think of listing as contributing to productivity we shall find one thing: improved human competence. And since human competence is a result of education, training and research the presumption is strong that these are the factors on which technical progress ultimately hinges'.

TABLE VII

Growth of Output in Western Countries

(compound annual percentage rates of growth of national product at constant prices)

COUNTRY	1929 to 1939	1939 to 1949	1949 to 1959	1929 to 1959 (Average) (1)—(3)
Canada	0·6	5·5	4·2	3·4
Western Germany	4·3	2·2	7·4[1]	3·2
Sweden	3·0	3·0[2]	3·4	3·1
Norway	3·2	2·4	3·4	3·0
Finland	3·1	1·6	4·2	3·0
United States	0·6	4·4	3·3	2·8
Italy	1·6	0·1	5·9	2·5
Netherlands	0·4	2·3	4·8	2·5
Denmark	2·5	1·5	3·2	2·4
Switzerland	0·1	1·5[3]	5·2	2·2
Austria	0·6[4]	0·8[2]	6·0	2·1
United Kingdom	2·2[5]	1·0[2]	2·4	1·9
Spain	1·7[6]	1·1[7]	5·2	1·5
France	1·1	1·1	4·5	1·2
Belgium	0·2[5]	0·6[2]	3·0	1·1
Greece	—	2·0	5·9[3]	1·9[8]

Source: 'Economic Survey of Europe 1961, Part II' (United Nations)

[1] 1950 to 1959   [4] 1928 to 1937   [7] 1940 to 1949
[2] 1937 to 1949   [5] 1929 to 1937   [8] Average of two
[3] 1938 to 1949   [6] 1929 to 1940   decades.

This highlights one of the chief causes for concern in Europe, namely the lack of communication between industry and university. This is one of the major causes of the brain drain and of the gap in knowledge between Europe and America. For Europe to regain her former standing in the world, she will have to make maximum use of her 'educational residual'—which, in essence, is the greatest capital on earth.

Two fundamentals on which we feel any plan for relief of the current trends in the brain drain should rest, are a *balanced* development, and preparedness to compete in tomorrow's markets.

Building universities and organizing them to feed industry are essential parts of the plan, but whilst vitally important, they are not sufficient in themselves. Young engineering and science graduates will not be prepared to stay in a country without a progressive research and industrial platform on which to build their careers. The top graduates from the leading countries in Europe are not the sort of people who, having worked hard and achieved mental satisfaction at their universities, will tolerate half-success or half-fulfilment in their subsequent careers.

Today universities and research institutions are overcrowded with traditional stumbling blocks which are completely incompatible with the spirit of research. Moreover the growing demands of research cause these stumbling blocks to become more obstructive every day.

Only 15 per cent of those men and women qualified to teach in primary schools have had any formal education in science. This lack of interest will undoubtedly be reflected in their pupils' secondary school interests and choice of careers. For science does not come easily to the young unless it is taught by people who are interested in it. The way to remove this first stumbling block, therefore, is to insist on a certain minimum of science instruction at teachers' training colleges.

The Second French National Symposium at Caen[1] agreed that, in future, universities should under no circumstances maintain the 'feudal system' of chairs, and that all students able to follow university education should be welcome to do so. The European educational system has until now been more concerned with short-term tactics than long-term strategy, and has been keen rather to express than to shape tradition. It has been more preoccupied with present status than with speculation about the pattern of the future.

The Caen symposium issued a fifteen-point pronouncement which we firmly believe should form the basis for a charter for university reconstruction in every corner of Europe:

[1] Held in the autumn of 1966.

1 Creation of experimental public, autonomous universities not divided into faculties.

These universities should have the power to develop their own study and research programmes, to supersede the present uniform, centralized universities in metropolitan centres. They should be competitive and diversified.

2 The status of public institution (with scientific and technological connotations) to be conferred on the universities and the research establishments.

This status should assure the flexibility of functioning accorded to business and industrial concerns.

3 Replacement of the system of professional chairs dominating the various disciplines by a system of academic departments. The faculty professors would thus become general university professors.

The breakdown of the watertight faculty chairs to allow a regrouping of disciplines was proposed by Nobel biochemist Jacques Monod, and enthusiastically supported by the conference.

4 Limitation of the number of students at each university to a reasonable figure, perhaps 20,000.

This would lead to the construction of some fifteen individual universities in the Greater Metropolitan Paris region, and several universities in the provincial towns and cities.

5 Regrouping of the currently existing faculties into teaching departments and research institutes, each presided over by a man elected for a finite period of time.

6 Nomination of university professors on the basic of scientific criteria, independently of titles.

7 The research institutes to recognize the need for calling upon a variety of forms of financial assistance.

8 The launching of new endeavours concentrated on fundamental research and on a pan-European basis.

9 Completion of the hospital and university medical school reform currently in progress, with special emphasis on medical research.

10 Determination of a programme of research based on long-term planning and associating university with industry.

The execution of this programme would be effected through research contracts between industry and university authorities, observing the principles of industrial propriety.

11 Increasing the means and improving the methods of technical demonstration, information retrieval being an indispensable tool for research.

12 Society should give to any young man of any age, and at any level of general studies, the means of taking up a profession.

13 Teachers to develop a systematic counselling of all students and their families particularly concerning choice of career.

14 Revision of the present system of training elementary and high-school teachers of all specializations and degrees, who should receive not only academic knowledge but also a psycho-sociological and professional training.

15 Higher education should be oriented towards accepting the idea of life-long learning.

This is a thoughtful pronouncement of able men who can read tomorrow's newspaper and plan for the future. Its foresight is such that we can add nothing to it. A society undergoing change needs a philosophy, and this is the one we would offer to the universities of Europe.

DEVELOPING HUMAN RESOURCES

One could say that the necessity for massively financed research has long been recognized but that the thorny question has always been 'Who pays?' Industry will not usually extend research beyond the scope of its own particular markets; universities are often ill-equipped and understaffed and working in isolation from manufacturing and marketing guidance; and governments are naturally reluctant to hand over vast sums for research which may be wasted or even misappropriated.

The answer to these problems can be demonstrated by way of examples. In America there are some 450 research organizations concerned with advanced technology, engineering and science. Many of these are non-profitmaking and since the end of World War II have dominated scientific progress in the West. It may be useful to describe some of the more important of these non-profitmaking organizations to emphasize the importance to Europe of 'thinking big' when planning the economic future.

The oldest and the most important of these institutions is the RAND Corporation. It works principally for the Air Force, the Office of the Secretary of Defence, and the National Aeronautics and Space Administration. RAND was established in 1946 (as Project RAND) and it is best known for its studies of strategic warfare. In 1954, its analyses helped get the United States intercontinental ballistic missile programme started.

A study of the analytical research projects carried out by RAND, and of their contribution to dispelling some of the 'idea illusions' of so many researchers and executives, can be revealing in itself, and RAND has been impressive in its determination to avoid over-expansion in fields which are not its own. RAND was instrumental in the establishment of two other non-profitmaking organizations which act as magnets for intellect, the Systems Development Corporation and Analytic Services.

Systems Development budded from RAND in 1956, through RAND's reluctance to involve itself in hardware development; it evolved from RAND's work on the Semi-Automatic Ground Environment air defence system. Analytic Services was created in 1958 at the advice of RAND, to give the Air Force staff greater capacity in analysing tactical problems, compared with strategic problems which were RAND's speciality.

One might ask why an all-European RAND-type organization entrusted with the continent's survival has not yet been formed. Regrettably, the main reason is that governments are too fearful of relinquishing their autonomy and sharing prestige with other countries, though the contribution that RAND has been able to make to American security shows what could be done for Europe.

An organization with similar aims to RAND is the Institute for Defence Analysis. This is used by the Joint Chiefs of Staff and the Director of Defence Research and Engineering. Founded in 1956 by a consortium of five universities headed by Massachusetts Institute of Technology,[1] IDA has been greatly aided by Ford Foundation Grants. IDA basically functions, through its Weapons Systems Evaluation Division, as a high-level, long-range study group. A second Institute division serves the State Department and the Arms Control and Disarmament Agency.

The Logistics Management Institute, established in 1961, is responsible to the Assistant Secretary of Defence for Installations of Logistics, and to the three military logistics staff elements. Studies range from the 're-programming' of the logistics computer according to cost/efficiency criteria, to more generic undertakings on subjects expected to respond to analytical treatment.

The Centre for Naval Analyses, chartered in 1962 under the auspices of the Franklin Institute, is a long-range study organization with only limited responsibility for contemporary analysis. Like the Logistics Management Institute, this organization is too new to have had a major impact on Defence programmes, but its potential should not be underestimated.

The Army's Research Analysis Corporation was born out of controversy in 1961, after the Army had refused to accept some recommendations of the Operations Research Office, of Johns Hopkins University. Research Analysis Corporation is actually the Operations Research Office reconstituted separately from Johns Hopkins. It has studied tactical and logistical problems of the Army

---

[1] In 1968, this membership has been shaken because of IDA's involvement in research efforts.

and assessed some of the strategic problems involved in the development of an anti-missile system. Systems Development grew out of RAND in 1956, as a result of the demand for hardware and software developments. Within the broader horizons of systems engineering, three other organizations deserve a mention. These are the MITRE Corporation, the Applied Physics Laboratory (Johns Hopkins University), and the Aerospace Corporation.

Originally, the MITRE Corporation developed from the reluctance of MIT to become involved in long-range systems engineering, particularly in connection with SAGE.[1] The necessary long term requirements of the Department of Defence were responsible for the establishment of this non-profitmaking systems engineering firm. MITRE, by gaining the confidence of the military, has access to information that could never be made available to a contractor.

Working along similar lines, the Applied Physics Laboratory (of Johns Hopkins University) first started systems research for the Navy in the 1940s as part of the 'Bumblebee' Project. The objective was to investigate the feasibility of guided missiles. The surface-to-air family of missiles, Tartar, Terrier, and Talos, evolved from this group of studies. The Laboratory now provides systems engineering and technical direction of Navy missile and space programmes.

The Aerospace Corporation grew out of the Space Technology Laboratories. STL was established in 1954 by Ramo-Wooldridge to oversee development of America's first intercontinental ballistic missiles: Atlas, Titan, and Minuteman. Pioneered by the military, non-profitmaking research organizations have proliferated and now include such diverse agencies as the National Institute of Health, the Federal Aviation Agency, NASA, and the Atomic Energy Commission.

It is obvious that the non-profitmaking organizations have played a tremendously important role in American research but they have by no means carried the entire burden. American industry has long recognized the need for incentives, or inducements, to attract and

---

[1] Semi-Automatic Ground to Air Equipment, for defence of air space.

then retain the highest scientific talent. Its scientists, engineers and managers are encouraged to pursue private research towards advanced degrees. Many companies go much further. The Bell Laboratories, for instance, give extensive aid to those of their staff who wish to publish their research, offering them time off to write papers and books, even offering editorial assistance.

The whole country benefits as well as the individual companies. Not only does this attractive condition of employment help Bell to build up a team of high talent, it also encourages its scientists to keep in touch with the outside world. In 1965, Bell staff delivered over 2000 lectures and talks.

Most European companies shy away from the risk of 'leakage' in this system, but Bell reckon there is no better way of making a research laboratory a centre of new ideas. And although Bell has staffed the top scientific posts in a number of important universities, especially in the field of solid state physics, its own brain drain in an intensely competitive world is only two per cent a year.

To compare this courteous and professional treatment of scientists with the way they are regarded in Europe would be funny were the situation not so depressing and dangerous. There is not even the excuse that this whole issue has taken European leadership by surprise. Although the expression 'Brain Drain' has been in use only a very few years, and the public at large have been aware of the problem only a little longer, nevertheless its dangers have been foreseen since at least the early 1950s. Furthermore, there has been great attention focused on the brain drain in more recent years and a mass of advice proffered in newspapers and business journals.

It is all the more strange, therefore, that no positive step has been taken to develop our manpower resources in the required direction. There is no mystery about it; the main issues are clear to any person who keeps informed on the subject. And the publication of the Jones Report, while welcome as a means of attracting wider attention to the brain drain, can have yielded few surprises. Its findings were, it would be fair to say, known in advance—and its specific hard-core recommendations cannot be said to be its major asset.

The problem is nothing if not urgent; months, let alone years, should not be allowed to drift by. This is true even if nowhere in the Jones Report's list of 'around the issue' suggestions is there a single word to indicate the urgency of the solutions it advises. We consider this a fault in the Report, an extremely unfortunate one considering the natural inertia of government departments and their propensity for talking over problems rather than getting things done.

Any move would require planning but some moves could be made quicker than others. If it would take one year to evolve a comprehensive policy for the better development of our human resources, let us initiate some immediate action in each European country to carry us through that year, so that at least the problem has not grown, while the plan is being drawn up, beyond its terms of reference.

With this object in mind we propose the immediate setting up of several non-profitmaking research organizations on the American pattern. Let us not consume a vast amount of time in the application of red tape: no great planning would be required for this purely stop-gap measure, as it is required to operate only during the period of policy planning and the subsequent initiation of the policy's requirements. We would hope that the formulation of a comprehensive, all-European policy would take not longer than one year, and a further four years for it to be fully operational.

One would hope that the cost of these non-profitmaking research centres would be recovered many times in terms of the results they would produce. But even if the costs were not so recovered and the money spent had to be written off, here is what would be gained: research centres functioning for five years plus whatever material results emerged; motivation towards the realization of a European policy; and, most important of all, a pool of talent immediately available to the policy as soon as it swung into action.

PART III

TOWARDS NEW HORIZONS

Chapter Nine

THE UNIVERSITY/INDUSTRY
RELATIONSHIP

'Reading makes a full man; conference a ready
man; writing an exact man.'   Francis Bacon

Investment in research and development is justified, if for no other
reason, if it attracts and retains brain power. The sort of research
which would stem the brain drain must be preceded by the creation
of the appropriate environment: a challenging environment in
which a man of high calibre would find it profitable and pleasant
to live and work. Scientists and technologists are single-minded
about their needs in life, and there is nothing more disheartening
to the new graduate than the knowledge that his country is unable
to offer the proper creative environment.

The environment the United States has created is based upon
twenty years of immense post-war government spending in research
and development. It has been suggested that America's discovery
of the enormous economic advantages of higher education was
largely accidental, that circumstances forced it upon them. But no
one can deny that, having discovered the fact, they exploited it
brilliantly. As a senior executive was to remark during our discussion in London: 'Planning and control, in the sense I am using
it, means the American approach to university curricula, to close
university/industry collaboration and to massively sponsored research (both by government and by industry) at the university site.'

It is no accident that science-based industries in America are
growing up around the university campuses, to form a new kind of
city—the 'ideopolis' or 'city of intellect'. This situation is in some
ways reminiscent of the eighteenth century's Industrial Revolution

when factories grew up around coal and iron ore deposits, seaports, and the like. The industries of the future will congregate around centres of learning in order to exploit their principal raw material, intellectual talent.

This knowledge should be enough to make city councils, industries and governments extremely alarmed that, of the scientists earning graduate degrees in a particular area, only a few stay to work there. The intense economic growth of some American cities and areas can be explained by the strength of their local knowledge industries. For example, over the last ten years thirty new companies have established themselves in Austin, Texas, making use of the ability supplied by the local university. Each of its 27,000 students costs the state of Texas $1500 per year, but the state regards this expense as adequately compensated by the boom in industry attendant upon the university's existence.

During 1966, the largest slice of US defence outlays went to California: this is America's most go-ahead state with the greatest investments in education and research. Californian companies in the state took in $5·8 billion in prime contracts, more than double the total amount going to firms in New York state. But how many European state or provincial governments are prepared to spend vast sums on research and education before there is a booming industry? They prefer to sit and wait for industry to raise itself from nothing and then cast around for the talent to keep it going.

To increase the investment return on human intellect, American states are now experimenting with new structures for the academic year. The change to a trimester system in California, undertaken primarily to save money, will produce an estimated $333 million saving in construction costs by 1975. Should the trimester plan succeed in spreading the student load, it might be followed ultimately by new schedules for both elementary and high schools. Already summer classes at these levels are becoming important in urban America. In the old rural society, classes used to shut down in summer so that all hands could help to bring in the crops, but this has no application in present-day urban societies.

Certain areas in a country may develop fast at the expense of other areas. In the United States, for instance, California is far and away the leader; in greater Los Angeles and greater San Francisco, there are more than 600 science-oriented firms, and in the first five years of the 1960s California managed to acquire an impressive 38·5 per cent of Federal R & D funds. This, in turn, led to the critical shortage of engineers which hit the West Coast in early 1966. The Knowledge Revolution is thus changing the economic geography of the nation. Because the dominant 'growth' institutions of the future will be not the factories but the 'intellectual organizations', the centres of progress and wealth will tend to merge. The research corporations, the industrial laboratories, and the leading universities, will attract industry and manpower, and thereby influence provincial growth.

Europe should take note of American education policy, particularly as it is shaped in California. The impetus behind the Californian investment has been the belief in the long-term importance of a sound and profitable educational/economic co-operation.

The most forward-looking provision of the programme has been the expansion of educational research and development, particularly in such areas as teaching techniques and curriculum improvement. Also significant has been the establishment of a complementary system of government insured and subsidized loans for children of middle-income families; and the expansion of existing work-study programmes which also help students meet college costs.

The question of the relevance of curricula is a key one. In several countries, the university system is so outdated that the students and their tutors are using textbooks considered obsolete in industry ten years ago. That bites deeply into efficiency standards. The attitude of European industries towards university curricula will have a decisive effect on the future course of the brain drain. We were delighted to hear that the Confederation of British Industries has recently set up a special committee to investigate the extent to which university curricula match industry's needs. This is a worthwhile step, provided first that industry itself

knows what it needs. One important question that must be settled is whether the young generation should be trained in a general way to use their minds or should be trained in specific skills.

Mr Kerr-Muir, a director of Courtaulds, stated in the course of our discussion that if a man is trained to learn he can easily pick up the skills as he gains experience in his work. Skills were usually most essential during the first year of industrial life, but as a man progresses in his career the depth of his background shows up. Within a rapidly changing environment in which technology progresses through great leaps, skills soon become obsolete, and then the most useful man is the one who has learned to adapt quickly and smoothly to new processes.

It is essential that enough graduates are produced with the right sort of skills. Few European universities have kept up with the new technologies, or have the appropriate staffs for doing so. They are not training the computer men and the systems analysts that management needs and would employ, and as a director was to remark: 'Nor do they provide the courses necessary for the retraining and upkeep of their current stock of industrial executives.'

We admit that it is by no means easy for governments to estimate future supply and demand of scientists. And we have in fact stated repeatedly that this cannot be done very effectively without a comprehensive planning of industry's future. But it is both hideously expensive and irrational to keep on producing skills nobody needs while industry is disastrously short of other skills.

A French executive said that much of the blame for misguided thinking lies with the Ministry of Education: 'Roughly, what it does is right; and, unquestionably, the way it does it is wrong.' In October 1966 French universities opened with a record-breaking enrolment of a little over half a million, in a country of forty-nine million people. The ratio is impressive, but Ministry of Education officials admitted that despite their efforts they had not been able to persuade enough students to enter the fields in which France most desperately needs university-trained specialists: science and engineering.

The government's efforts to woo more students into technical studies during 1966 produced an increase of only seven per cent. As this figure was less than the percentage increase in all students, it represented a relative decline. In the same year, students in law and economic sciences increased by fifteen per cent, and those in the liberal arts by eleven per cent. It is hollow comfort that the disappointingly small number of technical students reduces the pressure on another area of deficiency, namely the number of professors available in the sciences.

France and many other European countries have rightly committed themselves to ambitious programmes for expanding and modernizing the teaching of science. But, the programmes having been planned in detail, it has been discovered that the hardest thing to do is to find enough professors up to date with scientific progress. As a result plans have never materialized. Students are fed with the same old stuff, and the malaise can be expected to continue for a long time.

Our research in Britain in particular brought to light a widening gap between the training that the universities give, and the use made in industry of that training. We were surprised at the extent of misunderstanding about what a university-trained man should actually do, and at the widespread feeling among young graduates that they were 'under-employed'. Considerable waste ensues if brainpower is misemployed and under-utilized. In addition, further emigration is encouraged.

The employment of science graduates is not of course without its difficulties. A complaint often voiced among industrial executives is that a university graduate joining a company will ask 'When am I going to be managing director?' But these executives should be delighted at the enterprise and ambition displayed. Science graduates are the most prone to feel that they are intellectually superior to the managers who direct them, and may resent the fact that in Europe a science degree provides them with a much less promising start on the route to a directorship than it does in the United States. It is true that a scientist must be prepared to divert himself from the centre of his own particular field if he is to succeed in management, but he will be no less useful directing the work of others from first-hand background experience.

The American approach to education, and the close link in the US between university and industry, has created a situation there where the science graduate's chances of becoming managing director or president are far higher than they are in Europe.

We have said a lot about America, but nobody should underestimate Russia's concentrated and efficient effort in the field of ability. Russia is also converting its economy from one based on natural resources to one based on human resources. In 1959 Frank Pace, Jr, then President of General Dynamics Corporation, warned in an issue of *Fortune* magazine against underestimating Russia's capacity to concentrate in specific areas:

'If the area has real military or psychological value to them, they'll put massive concentration on it, and achieve results out of all proportion to the general level of their technical ability.'

Russia is in no position at the present to drain off talent from Western Europe, but we should take note of the efforts of Russia and America if we intend to stop the brain drain and bridge the knowledge gap. And who can be sure that tomorrow Russia or even Japan will not be active in the brain market, absorbing the best in grey matter from the other continents?

If Europe is to keep her most able men, she will have to provide them with adequate facilities for further education of all kinds. The success of a nation will depend ultimately on its proportion of able and trained men, and this is why we stress the importance of educational opportunity. Mr McNamara expressed a similar view during a discussion on the brain drain when he said, 'Europe is weak educationally. That weakness is severely crippling its growth. It is weak in its general education and in its technical education.'

Robert Major[1] has laid particular emphasis on the outstanding

[1] Director of the Royal Norwegian Council for Scientific and Technical Research.

long-term approach of the American research effort. He places education next to able forecasting and planning in order of importance:

'Pretty soon, every human being will have to spend some twenty-five per cent of his productive life in education. But education, like research, should be forward looking and planned appropriately. Here lies a good deal of the difference between Europe and the United States. Europe has not yet adopted the forward look and it is correct to add that the gap in Europe is not in pure technology but in management and in markets.

'If you talk to basic researchers working in European laboratories they invariably complain about the lack of governmental support. In so doing they forget the all important ingredients of 'go-spirit' and management skill. What European industry needs most is the sort of high-calibre managers who have both the ability to forecast and the personality to steer a course of action towards fruitful results.'

In Major's opinion, the drive towards change should start at the university level. 'The universities themselves,' he said, 'are awfully slow in making changes. As a result, the Royal Norwegian Council for Scientific and Technical Research now works through the students rather than the university authorities. It helps them understand their own interests and encourages them to press the universities to change.'

Norwegian industry has in fact been fairly progressive in changing its attitude towards scientific personnel. But there was a time, in the pre-war period, when scientists and engineers had minimal scope in Norwegian industry. Professor Birger Bergersen, who was Minister of Education when the Technical University at Trondheim was built, told us that in the 1930s nearly all Trondheim graduates left for America because they could find no work in Norway. At that time Trondheim's Technical University was known in some circles as the 'Norwegian-American Line'. European industry has got to understand the need of its top scientists, engineers and technologists to continue their research studies after graduation.

A Norwegian engineer who obtained his post-graduate degree in the United States and spent a few years working there, was most critical of the total lack of post-graduate studies in his country of origin:

'I got my Master's in Pittsburgh and the company for which I was working paid everything for me and gave me free time to complete some of my credit courses. This kind of company reaction does not exist in Norway. Practically nothing is being offered in the way of assistance for the development of scientists. In order to undertake doctoral studies I have to emigrate.'

A similar outcry about the total lack of a well-reasoned post-graduate programme came from many other scientists in Europe, particularly from those who had spent some years in the United States and then returned to their country of origin. A university Reader in Electrical Engineering, who worked for some years in America before returning to England, had this to say:

'... During the time I worked at (a company in America) on eddy current couplings the kind of work that I was being encouraged to do was of sufficiently high calibre to be submitted to a British university for the degree of Ph.D. ... and the Company gave me every possible encouragement to submit this work. ... Whereas in my present job (in England) I have the greatest difficulty in persuading British industry to release people for higher degrees, the exact opposite was true in America and (the Company) had excellent schemes to encourage their engineers to work for Master's and Doctor's degrees, and last year I heard of a B.Sc. who went to America with a guarantee that he would be allowed to continue his studies to Ph.D. level in the local university, in addition to receiving an excellent starting salary from the firm.' [1]

The change must be one of philosophy and total outlook. The

[1] Quoted from the Jones Report.

organization of a few courses, or even of a few institutes will not change matters appreciably and produce the necessary integration of university and industry. Two years ago, the Business Economics Institute in Oslo sensed a need for developing systems analysis and tested the opinions of Norwegian companies on the wisdom of establishing a one-year's systems analysis course. The initial reaction was most enthusiastic, indicating that between fifty and seventy men might attend. But when the course was organized and places were offered, only five men came forward and it had to be cancelled.

It is vital that European countries set to work at once to create the correct symbiotic university/industry relationship. These two vital sectors of the economy cannot continue to operate in separate ivory towers. Modern industry is science-based, and teamwork in scientific research and development must be encouraged. Only in this way can we produce scientists with management skills and managers who know how to exploit to the full the scientific research facilities that are available. Further scientific education *within* industry must be promoted, while university research workers must be motivated to look beyond the boundaries of their pure science.

Chapter Ten

STRATEGY BEFORE TACTICS

'Before encouraging swimmer to dive, one must first fill pool with water.'

Attributed to Confucius

On December 14, 1967, we submitted to the Minister of Technology, at the Ministry's request, a letter summarizing our thoughts and findings on management, technology, and more specifically on computer perspectives in Britain. These findings reflected three months' research which brought us in close contact with nearly 100 organizations, ministries, universities, research institutions and major industries. Our report underlined what we consider to be the four main deficiencies in the British industrial set-up.

1. *Failure to plan.* It was unpleasantly surprising to find throughout our research that planning is not a strong subject. This criticism is equally valid at governmental level and at company level—with very few exceptions among the large industrial corporations. Failure to plan is particularly apparent where the medium-to-long range is concerned.

2. *Failure to bridge the gap between R & D and marketing.* British scientists have led the world with many basic discoveries, but Britain has not been able to successfully exploit these discoveries in world markets. On the contrary, original ideas have fled from Britain to other lands, to return some years later to their country of origin as products of a foreign technology.

3. *Failure to appreciate the university graduate and his knowhow.* This is a serious failure, and time runs out fast. Britain urgently needs to kill three birds with one well-placed stone: (a) remove the wall separating the universities from industry; (b) utilize university

students properly in industry; (c) make industry pay and treat the university graduate as it should.

4. *Failure to provide incentives*. No one supposes that people will work harder without incentives; that industries will invest in modernization without the reward of profits; that the government will get any mileage out of an economy which runs out of steam. Without incentives, risk-taking is almost non-existent, and as Lord Waverley once said of Sir Winston Churchill: 'After all, if he'd been cautious and had taken no risks he would have been of less use to us.'

These four major deficiencies are clearly responsible for a working environment in Britain which encourages able and entrepreneurially-minded men to seek opportunities elsewhere. This point need not be laboured. But these are deficiencies in the *working* environment. What about domestic ties?

One of the current myths is that highly skilled men will return to their countries of origin *en masse*, influenced by emotional and domestic considerations. Not that a few would not return because of genuinely feeling that they owe their country of origin more in the way of service than they have been prepared to give until now. But these are a few. Also few are the Europeans, particularly northern Europeans, in America yearning for typically home-country pursuits, social events, food and familiar scenery. However, Mr H. S. Hoff of the Joint Recruiting Board does believe that the reasons for return are largely familial:

'The reasons the migrants want to come back are domestic in the main. One, they want to come back to be within reach of elderly parents in this country. Two, they want to have their children educated in this country. Also, wives do not settle down so well— thank God for British wives! It is jolly good if a young scientist marries his girl before he goes, because if he puts it off and marries an American girl, then we say goodbye to him for good. The scientific world is still mainly peopled from the lower middle classes, and the sort of girls they marry are nurses, teachers, secretaries; or girls who are in the same social class as themselves. On the whole, such girls want to return to "Mum's country".'

But can it be seriously thought that a brain gain policy can be based on the emotional reaction of housewives. Undoubtedly a small number of emigrants will return for these reasons. But most of the evidence shows that those who try to *induce* emigrants to return are on a difficult wicket. The difficulty obviously is the character of the *total* environment in Europe—in which the *working* environment is a key component. In the past few years there have come into being a number of recruiting campaigns, some sustained and some spasmodic, to persuade European scientists working in America to return home. Most people would agree that these campaigns can be only a temporary measure and that they are tackling the problem from the wrong end. Optimists would say that even if these campaigns do not produce immediate physical results it is excellent that our young scientists and engineers are reminded of our interest in them.

The first organized recruiting campaign of British origin, regarded as an only mildly successful but nevertheless sustained effort, came from the Joint Interviewing Board set up by the UK Atomic Energy Authority and the Civil Service Commission in 1958. This was later joined by the Central Electricity Generating Board. The Board is run by Mr H. S. Hoff. Recruiting is mainly in the lower grades (B.A.s and Ph.D.s under thirty), the reason being that it is generally considered more profitable to fill higher posts from men already within a company.[1]

The first approach is generally made through newspaper advertising and direct contact with the universities, and applicants interested in returning to Britain are invited to an interview. During the year April 1966 to April 1967 Mr Hoff's committee interviewed 200 young men as opposed to fifty in the first year of the scheme.

[1] An argument which has its merits, but is often used as a cover-up for expediency and inertia.

The record of the Joint Interviewing Board so far is given in Table VIII.

TABLE VIII

North American Joint Interviewing Board
Number of Interviews, Posts Offered and Posts Accepted

Year	No. of persons interviewed[1]	No. of persons recommended for appointment[1]	No. of persons receiving offers[1]	No. of persons accepting appointment	SRC (formally DSIR/NATO) fellowships
1958	45	37	Not known	7	—
1959	90	55	,,	17	—
1960	145	145	,,	21	11
1961	186	154	86	34	18
1962	244	165	101	53	18
1963[2]	236	146	75	20	19
1964	269	194	167	55	32
1965	247	194	145	44	40
1966	188	133	97	56	—

Source: Jones Report

[1] These figures include candidates accepting DSIR/NATO (subsequently SRC) Fellowships 1960–1965 inclusive. Since 1966 these Fellowships have been awarded without interview by the North American Boards.

[2] In 1963 the Central Electricity Generating Board joined the scheme.

It will be seen that an average seventy per cent of those interviewed are suitable for consideration and sixty per cent are offered jobs by one of the three organizations Mr Hoff represents. The names of those candidates for whom employment cannot be found immediately are passed on to other British institutions who might be interested, but it is believed that these elicit very little response. Of those men who are offered positions at home about three-sevenths accept. This figure may at first seem rather low. It is not necessarily so, and our comments would have been favourable if it were not for the fact that the number of those returning is but a very small fraction of those leaving.

There exists also the effort in the private sector. Other recruiting campaigns are run by Britain's industrial giants—ICI, Shell, and Unilever, and about fifteen others from time to time. ICI have sent a mission to the United States each year since 1960 and have recruited 120 people. Unilever have been recruiting in America since 1964 and about forty people have finally accepted jobs with them in Britain.

As is the case with the public sector, while this could be considered a gratifying result for the firms themselves, the figures are too small to have any appreciable effect on Britain's economic situation as a whole. The total recruitments of the Joint Interviewing Board, ICI, Shell, Unilever and all the other companies who are fishing in American waters comes nowhere near to equalling the number of scientists, engineers and technologists undertaking the opposite journey, and Britain's brain drain continues with only a slightly perceptible slowing down.

Canada has a system instituted in 1964 named Operation Retrieval. Its purpose is similar to Britain's Joint Interviewing Board, and keeps Canadian expatriate students informed about career opportunities at home in academic, governmental and industrial fields. Operation Retrieval is sponsored jointly by the academic community and the government. Like British graduates, Canadian ones tend to lose touch with developments in their own country pretty soon after leaving it.

During 1966 seven teams, composed mainly of academic personnel, visited Canadians working in universities and industries in the United States and Europe. The conclusions reached were that graduate students were grateful for the interest taken in them, they were out of touch with opportunities at home, and discouraged by the lack of response to letters sent to Canadian employers. Although they were being actively courted by American employers, a majority were prepared to return home *if* provided with a suitable opening. In this *if* lies the key to the whole problem. Job hunting at a distance is difficult.

One British Ph.D. who had been in the USA for five years reported to the Jones Working Group:

'I have no personal experience of applying for university posts in England. However, the consensus opinion of Britons here is that it is impossible to obtain a teaching position in England from here. The attitude seems to be that the person concerned must return to England and then take his chances . . .'

It seems that the methods employed by British groups who attempt to woo back emigrants from the USA are not always as perfect as they might be. The same British Ph.D. chemist told the Jones committee:

'To read the British Press one would imagine that a highly intensive campaign is being waged to get expatriate Britons to return. . . . I have received a single communication from . . . and I am currently on the . . . mailing list. The only face to face contact involved two representatives of . . . which was not a very happy experience. . . . They let me know in no uncertain terms their opinion of scientists who left for the money-pots of America and I heatedly told them what they could do. . . . Afterwards I felt somewhat contrite but not when I received a letter from head office advising me that my application for employment had been carefully considered and rejected!'

Moralizing about loyalty is clearly no answer to the current situation. The British recruiting campaigns launched in the USA are producing relatively insignificant results and are no part of a plan to eradicate the basic causes of the Anglo/US brain drain. They are tactical moves in a situation where strategy is the essential requirement. There can also be more than a suspicion that many of those emigrants who do return from the USA are merely people who have failed in the more competitive US environment.

Neither loyalty nor domestic ties can be relied on. The basic European problem is the creation of an attractive working environment for its talent. Against the background of such an environment, foreign recruiting excursions would be not merely successful, they would be unnecessary.

A young data-processing executive whom we met during our October/December 1967 research in Britain phrased as follows his reasons for leaving his country for America at the end of the year:

Britain is not getting anywhere and the disillusion of the younger generation increases every month.

Middle and higher management in industry as well as in Government are not interested in anything very much—except the preservation of the status quo.

America has become for the younger generation of British scientists, engineers and managers a sort of Western Frontier—and they want to see what it is like.

Those younger than forty know that their children will be at the peak of their careers in the year 2000—and these children may well be unable to grow. Even if I had no personal inducement to leave for America I would go for the sake of my children.

This makes depressing reading: and many may feel that it exaggerates the situation. Nevertheless, these opinions are commonly encountered and they are symptomatic of a basic dissatisfaction with the opportunities that are currently available in Britain. Some way must be found of creating a new 'Frontier' in Europe, offering the challenge and the excitement and the rewards which our current generation of graduates think they see across the Atlantic.

Chapter Eleven

THE MORIBUND COMMON
MARKET

*'Mon centre cède, ma droite recule, situation
excellente j'attaque.'*   Maréchal Foch

The greatest failure of the Common Market countries has been
their inability to manage the mechanism of growth. No management or marketing forces have yet developed sufficiently to exploit
Europe's inventive imagination. Apart from deficiencies of leadership, the community itself does not possess an adequate frame on
which to build. Europe's complacency about her own future has
become economically dangerous, and the immediate future of the
Common Market does not look hopeful.

The European Economic Community, EEC or the Common
Market, was founded by farsighted men who recognized that each
European country's interests were best served by association. But
the concept was not investigated deeply enough at the beginning,
and European governments and industries continue their failure to
grasp the real issues involved. The hope for Europe lies in able
management, a quality which is not, as yet, characteristic of the
Common Market alliance. As an attempt by European industry to
re-establish itself in the world market, the EEC has been remark-
ably unsuccessful, and much of the blame for this must be placed
on the absence of authoritative planning.

Many of the shortcomings of the Common Market have their
roots in the Treaty of Rome. Those who drew up the Treaty did
not foresee the requirements of research and development, and the
means (technological, human and financial) to make the best use of
it, and they also overestimated the degree to which industrial

integration would follow naturally from economic integration. The inadequacies of the Treaty of Rome are highlighted by the proliferation of American-based companies in Europe during the last ten years.

Certain European industries which once dominated world markets, such as German cameras, Swiss watches, British machine-tools, and French perfumes are now on the decline. It is estimated that by 1970 American companies will be producing half the cars in Europe, although it was not until 1959 that America started to take a serious interest in the European automobile market—with the exception of the investments made in the twenties when the automobile was a growing but hazy industry.

The European Economic Community seems to be an excellent institution for employing people, holding meetings and publishing reports, but it is uncertain whether in its present form it can ever play a central role in Europe's industrial, financial and technological development, let alone its political development. The reason for this failure lies in a framework too narrow for its objectives.

In its early years, the Common Market economy was the nearest approximation to that of America that analysts could find. But in the last ten years the American economy has clearly forged ahead of the Common Market countries. It has outstripped Western Europe in development and is quickly widening the gap. This view has eminent advocates in many places but somehow none seems to have the power to make the necessary bold moves.

Europe needs to take, above all, courageous action starting at the level of research and development. Europe, and the Common Market countries in particular, are placing too much emphasis on trivialities. This sort of attitude could easily accelerate the brain drain from Western Europe, for only farsighted planning of basic requirements will capture the imagination of the best men, and it is indisputable that at present Europe is finding it increasingly hard to recruit people for key posts.

The money for an industrial offensive in Europe is available; what is lacking is the sound planning and decision-making necessary to see it through. The fact that no European nation has yet been able to mount a great technological-industrial initiative is not only amazing, it is also tragic. Governments and managements have shown themselves unable to make clear and brave decisions for the long-term development of industry; if it has been fear of failure that has resulted in the present lack of long-term planning, then this is the end of Western Europe as an outstanding and autonomous entity.

It is not that men of calibre are missing; they still exist but somehow our system does not allow them to come to the surface. It is just another aspect of the same system which tends to exaggerate the trivial and to underestimate the crucial aspects of a European alliance. If Europe is to compete industrially with America at any time in the future it must take immediate steps to prevent its ablest young men emigrating to America: but positive steps rather than negative ones; incentives, not prohibitions.

Russia and America, with almost as many scientists and as much money invested in the science-based industries as all major European countries put together, are in a splendid position to keep their lead. To assail their position will require not only a visionary plan but the management ability to make swift adaptations of that plan as exigencies demand, both at the government level and in industry. For America and Russia will not be waiting to allow us to catch up, and the problems in five years time will not all be the same problems as today.

European industrialists and European governments must concentrate on essentials. If the objective is to regain leadership, governments must see that their collective rules and measures are able to provide a suitable institutional framework for such a strategy. We must realize that 'proportional growth' can no longer be achieved, and what Europe now needs is an ingenious strategy of unbalanced development. With finite human and material resources at its disposal, Europe would do best by aiming for one sector at a time.

It must be stressed that priorities must be ingeniously chosen, in the full understanding that betting on the future involves risks. We must work towards a European technological community because only the Continent's *combined* resources can stop the slide into 'second-class living'. Both the industrial inertia of Europe and the brain drain will continue as long as we fail to implement a long-term plan for political and economic integration.

Computers, aircraft, missiles, satellites, oceanology, and nuclear power production projects are the areas of industry in which we must fight the main battles. In the same line are components, machine tools, office equipment, petroleum, fertilizers, and chemicals. Multi-national corporations should be set up without delay to implement co-production in these industries. It would be an ambitious undertaking and would cost much in money, sweat and tears, but one effect it would immediately have would be to provide the conditions of employment sought by men who are currently emigrating. Expansion of European industry would bring with it increased opportunity for able men in all spheres of industrial life, particularly in research and development.

But not only must the opportunities be created, adequate financial and social rewards must accompany them. With a Europe which is healthy economically and politically a balanced brain drain could be achieved whereby Europe and America would lose brains to each other in equal proportions, and the transferring brains would gain an international outlook which would benefit their industrial, economic, and academic lives.

The American-based multi-national company is today larger in its resources and in its income than many single nations. The time has come to reconsider the role of European industry in this light. Other things being equal, the multi-national company is in the best position to use the mass approach to finance, research, development, manufacturing, marketing and personnel training and education.

Two policies are open to Europe in her future attitude towards the multi-national company. Either she must introduce a programme of equal partnership with the American enterprises; or she must institute European-based entities of colossal size which are capable of invading the American and Japanese markets.

In order to implement the first proposal, European industries would have to attract large-scale government investment. Only if the budget is enormous will the American companies feel they have something to gain from a programme of equal partnership. The second proposal involves nothing less than a complete merger of European companies; in finance, management, research, development, technology, industry, marketing, and, above all, in brain power. The merger, to be successful, must be complete and unambiguous at all levels. Either plan would do more than merely balance the brain drain, it would salvage European industry.

In November 1966 at the opening of Turin's Auto Show, Italy's foreign trade minister Guisto Tolley urged Europe's car builders to join forces to compete with American firms in world markets. He said:

'We are at the crossroads. The choice is either to create an industrial structure at European level within the framework of a Europe capable of competing in world markets, or resign ourselves to a subordinate role.'

Ability is the factor which in the future will be more crucial and far-reaching than any other. When the prestige of purely national industries is low, it is not surprising that multi-national companies are able to attract the best in brains. Nations are locally restricted, but the multi-national company has the means to acquire brains on a world scale.

With very few exceptions, European industries are not yet strong enough (and their countries of origin not wealthy enough) to mount a counter attack against America on their own. An example of a European multi-national concern is the European Coal and Steel Community. The Coal and Steel Community was for a long time considered to be a model for economic development; it promoted steel and coal production, cut tariffs, achieved fair pricing, and took much of the malice out of Franco-German industrial rivalry. Then, just when it ought to have been congratulating itself on its successes, the Community seemed to fall into disarray. In November 1966, the European Coal and Steel Community agreed in principle to new measures to assist the steel industry of the EEC. The French, however, were opposed to the system of subsidies proposed, the ultimate effect of which would be to reduce the price of coking coal.

The very reason for the existence of the Coal and Steel Community had been to treat the coal and steel problems of western Europe as a whole. Yet, as its president said in late 1966: 'Since June we have watched a development of replacing a community plan with dangerous and unacceptable national plans.' The harsh facts of marketing life shape reactions and results in this way; as long as national solutions or arguments over-ride European ones, multi-national European industries cannot survive.

The tragic thing, of course, is that, although Europe's main hope is the development of multi-national companies, they are unlikely to appear for some time. We do not believe that industrial integration can be carried very far without political and economical integration beforehand. At present, European countries have no unity in their financial thinking; their management traditions are too diverse; they are severely lacking in legislation to cover all-European companies; and their accounting practices are too diverse.

Successful integration implies more than just a merger. It demands the establishment of the same wavelength in management evaluation and decision. Today this common denominator does not exist. We were told by London bankers that during 1965 some twenty Italian companies were looking for a buyer in London—but no British financier trusted the books he was presented with well enough to engage in negotiations.

It is essential that discrepancies in Europe's managerial, legal and financial practice be ironed out as soon as possible, but we see little evidence that executives of the Common Market are taking the initiative in this respect. In Britain things are no better. It is as if the men responsible for Europe's future are determined to show continuing unwillingness to face economic, industrial, educational, and even political reality.

We have noted before in these chapters that, again and again, the American talent for productivity and marketing has exploited the inventions of Europe. Europeans have provided the creative talent, Americans the manufacturing ability. But let us not adopt the complacent attitude that we are the intelligent ones, and that the Americans are a bunch of uncouth, technological parasites trading on our celestial brainpower. We are in fact very stupid.

It is not enough to invent something. Invention is the first half of an obvious two-fold task—invention and application. To allow America to put our inventions into production, then sell them back to us while we are still celebrating our achievement, is the most costly brain drain of all.

At least when America receives immigrants from Europe she is getting only education and potential ability which it will cost money to realize. But when we carry the whole invention process up to production stage before letting America take it over we are not even giving them something for nothing—we are giving them something for nothing *and* leaving ourselves with a further net deficit in the future. The cost of educating the talent, of employing it, of setting up the processing machinery, of the distraction from other ventures, of the loss of the market, and of the frustration of talent, all contribute to making the technological gap yawn wider.

Unless we act very fast this is just what will happen in perhaps the most important industry of all: nuclear power. Britain used to lead the world in the production of nuclear power for conversion to electricity, and in the first ten years up to 1965 the scoreboard read: Britain, 61 billion kilowatt-hours; America, 21·6; Italy 8·7; France, 4·2.

But America has already outstripped Britain in production overseas. It has invested 1·3 billion dollars in research and development, and more than sixty per cent of the new generating capacity ordered by utility companies in 1966 was nuclear, as against twenty-two per cent in 1965. Production installations now being set up are in units large enough to light whole cities. Duke Power is building a $157 million plant that will generate 1,600 Mw; Commonwealth Edison is expanding its Dresden plant into 1800 Mw; and Virginia Electric and Power which initially ordered a 750,000 kilowatt plant changed its order to two 800,000 kilowatt plants.

Once a country can draw ahead in the race to produce plants acceptable overseas it has every chance of staying there, for the ability to see ahead will have a beneficial effect on costs. General Electric and Westinghouse have ceased to price their tenders on a one-off basis, on the known assumption that future orders for similar plants will enable them to recover their design costs over a number of years. And in turn, quantity production of standardized components for these plants in itself brings down the total cost.

One of the main reasons for the US advantage, according to a senior executive of the British Central Electricity Generating Board, is that the English system was designed for English conditions only, and is not the most convenient for the poorer developing countries to buy. It works on a 'low enrichment' principle, requiring a high capital investment which incurs low running costs, whereas the American systems follow the opposite pattern—lower capital investment, but more expensive fluid.

The brain drain from Britain's nuclear industry, as registered by the Atomic Energy Authority, has not been heavy, although in 1967 the Assistant Director of Harwell accepted a key post with the American Westinghouse Company. Of the Atomic Energy Authority's 1200 senior scientists, only twelve left the United Kingdom in the year ending April 1967, and it is very encouraging that not only did a similar number return, but some outstanding atomic scientists from the United States have come to work at Harwell and Culham. Nevertheless the future of these two establishments is in fact in some doubt, and it is feared in some circles that unless a rapid decision is made about their future role in Britain's nuclear power industry, there will be a sharp increase in the brain drain from this sector of the community.

For the next five years the most profitable course of action for

Europe might be an immediate Franco-British undertaking in nuclear power. This would help France's industry to get off the ground, and at the same time lower the cost of the British effort by halving R & D costs. Not only would this boost confidence in Britain's ability to operate successfully at the frontiers of knowledge, but it would be instrumental in plugging that particular brain drain before it starts. This should be done irrespective of Common Market policies, if necessary.

Another field in which Britain has retired before America's marketing onslaught is electronics. Affecting, as it does, practically every aspect of the economy, the electronic industry is a factor by which a nation's strength may well be measured. A go-ahead country should therefore have a solid and healthy electronics industry with its own research facilities. A dozen years ago Britain led the world in the production of computers; but now ninety per cent of computers installed in Europe are not British but American.

One of the fastest (if not the fastest) developing aspects of the electronics industry is that of information storage and retrieval. As an English industrial leader commented:

'By 1980, the twilight period between invention and production may have shortened. Far-reaching change will result from people having instant access through computers to an enormous accumulated fund of knowledge; knowledge which is now distributed in scores of laboratories and libraries and thousands of files, even in a single industrial organization. Systems of data retrieval will be widely established by 1980; and they will cover the whole field of a company's activities, not merely its technical data.'

Europe badly needs massive information systems knowhow which she can exploit in the world market. At the moment she is pouring money into the pockets of America by buying her machines. She is also neglecting the booming new key areas of applications analysis, software support, greyware manufacturing and systems design. Yet the computer industry is so important, both in terms of economics and of manpower, that European governments should be both willing and able to make big investment in the industry. Despite serious attempts by Britain and France to compete with America in the computer business, American research and production methods still remain at the forefront, and will continue to do so unless there is a serious, united European effort in the very near future.

This is the tragic story of this decade. On a *per capita* basis Britain leads the world in original inventions, but ironically it has got little in return except the brain drain. The problem of developing technology needs really long-term planning on all fronts, which the Common Market should have given us years ago. But the EEC countries have not yet learned to suborn their nationalist loyalties for the sake of the common good.

At the fiftieth anniversary dinner of the Association France–Grande Bretagne in Paris, the Duke of Edinburgh stressed the need to abandon national prejudice—the main stumbling block to a European union. EFTA and the Common Market should look for an integration of resources on a Europe-wide economic and industrial basis. 'The English,' he said, 'have been known to refer to the French as "frogs". I shall refrain from repeating what the French have been known to call the English.' But the French image of the English 'sitting around drinking tea in unheated houses, surrounded by permanent fog', described by the Duke, has to be dispelled along with a hundred other misleading and damaging images.

Much of what is wrong can be attributed to blindness in human imagination. This criticism applies not only to Britain and France, but to all the European countries in their relations with each other. A common market must have a common mind and a common identity of purpose. Europe is still full of national prejudice and that is one of the reasons why the Common Market has failed so far. England and the Continent desire the economic fruits of increasing prosperity all right, but both are reluctant to plant the necessary trees.

Chapter Twelve

WHITHER EUROPE?

'Genius is ninety per cent industriousness. The remaining ten per cent accounts for everything else.'   Helmut V. Moltke

Political stumbling blocks to European integration will not be removed merely by Britain's joining the Common Market or by any other measure which lacks far-reaching political insight. Aptly *The Economist* has said:

'So economic Europe, with or without Britain, will not be built in a day. Total integration of the market, giving firms the same chance to operate continent-wide as the Americans enjoy at home, will take many years. Indeed, technological advance via massive government contracts *à l'Américaine* will not be possible on anything like the American scale until a substantial degree of political, as well as economic, cohesion is achieved.'

Many informed men believe that the masters of Europe's political scientific and economic destinies should be subjected to stricter tests of accountability. They should be treated no differently from directors of the private industrial sector, and judged on the basis of established aims as against attained results. Realistic time schedules should be established and milestones fixed so that results achieved can be assessed against the established objectives and the money which has been spent.

Today's national boundaries are one target that could be tackled. Professor Eberhart Schmidt,[1] who believes that the major European

[1] General Manager, German Brown Boveri.

nations have not been able to make good use of their talent because of the splintered nature of Europe, asks:

'What is the explanation of the logic that there should be a whole dozen of leading nations in the world? I cannot imagine the present fractionation going on for another 2000 years. Day after day concepts of nationality become more meaningless until they will finally be exploded.'

We have stressed throughout this book that industrial integration of Europe should take place as soon as possible, and that this can hardly happen before the Continent is united politically and economically. It is now time to stress the value of a similar policy for education, not only at university level but starting right down in the primary school where learning of foreign languages is best begun.

The Common Market organization has made not the slightest move in this direction, so we once again advise that the natural good sense of all European countries (whether EEC members or not) be brought to bear on the problem. We should move towards a united educational policy even though the Common Market organization fails to undertake it. It is communications that will shape the new Europe, and without language integration communications cannot easily do their work.

Next comes the question of educational curricula. Here, isolated attempts at rationalization are taking place already. Our visit to the new site of Denmark's Technical University in Lungby revealed not only an impressive physical structure, but a new and dynamic curriculum. A ring of satellite Engineering Academies has been built throughout Denmark, whose graduates can continue studies for a higher level of specialization at the Technical University.

Copenhagen has made a welcome departure from nearsighted tradition, for universities today have a desperate need for industry-like effectiveness, and they in turn must help industry in the move towards concentration in high-technology fields. Not surprisingly, the bill for any such far-reaching policy is going to be high, but this would be justified even by a partial plugging of the brain drain let alone the rationalization of Europe's education policy.

The economic deficiencies of a country, of which the brain drain is one symptom, usually have their basis in education; and if educational systems are to be reformed and brought up to date it is obvious that brain power combined with the courage to evaluate alternatives and take the most favourable course of action are vital requirements. The problem is two edged, for not only do those countries which most desperately need a long-term educational policy lack the financial resources to implement it, but they have lost much of their invaluable human potential through the brain drain.

Europe suffers from educational problems which need rapid attention. The strains that exist in Europe are similar to those of emerging nations in that they have their basis, to a large extent, in problems of population. But this is not the whole story. Able men feel that opportunities for advancement in the teaching profession, both at school and university level, are greater in America than they are in Europe. This opportunity is both financial and structural. Until radical reform is made of the educational system, and especially of its wage structure, not only will the brain drain to other nations continue but there will be an internal drain away from the teaching profession.

Today there are approximately one million trained researchers, engineers and scientists in the world, but the requirement is expected to quintuple within eight years. This will far exceed the supply and therefore the brain drain can be expected to grow steadily worse. By 1975 the industrialized countries will share among themselves about 3·5 million scientists and engineers, leaving precious few for the remainder.

Within the next ten years, three-quarters of all men in industry are likely to be working on products quite unfamiliar to us today. Over the last few decades, the volume of the world's knowledge has far outstripped our capacity to absorb it and put it to work for us. This will result in tremendous wastage if we continue to ignore the advances needed in our educational programmes. Through lack of planning and failure to create progressive conditions the scientific, technological and economic gap between Europe and America will continue to widen until Europe awakes from its Rip Van Winkle sleep to learn the facts of life in the twentieth century.

Men must adapt themselves to the idea of continuing education throughout their working lives, the highly talented to further their knowledge, and the masses to adapt their skills to industry's varying needs. Continuous re-training and revising is in fact essential at all levels of the economy, but the onus does not lie with the individual; planning of these things must lie with governments, preferably a European government. The fate of Europe depends not only on whether she can keep her scientists and technologists, but also on whether she can educate her less skilled to play a meaningful part in industry. In all this, the Common Market should have given us a lead.

In 1967 a radical appraisal of England's defence and foreign policy led a group of Young Conservatives to conclude that 'commitment to Europe is at once our only choice and our greatest opportunity'. Their thesis was roughly this: Britain's military, economic and political interests compel her to try to enter the EEC: outside the Common Market, Britain would become more and more dependent on America, the Communist countries and South Africa. Their statement underlines the necessary long-term solution to the brain drain.

'That long dead myth of the special relationship between John Bull and Uncle Sam must finally be buried. . . . Outside the Common Market we can only expect the left-overs of capital from the US and elsewhere, and we shall have fewer of the techniques which American money in particular brings in its train.

'If we are to play any role in the world it must be within a community of European nations which would form an equal partnership with the United States.'

However, the acceptance of even the fundamentals of a plan

for Europe by its member nations is a major hurdle. When World War II ended, Britain was triumphant and was regarded as the equal of America and Russia. She had an excellent chance to lead Europe purposefully into the 1950s but let it go by. None of Europe's post-war leaders has been able to accept the fast-developing challenge; none has been able to face the pressure groups which, through ill-conceived personal interests, are bringing European development to a halt.

If Europe does not move fast it could easily become a technological backwater. An American calculation shows that within ten years some three-quarters of Europe's science-based, modern industries may be US-owned. It is conceivable that 90 per cent of the profits distributed from the sales achieved by these industries will by then be distributed to shareholders across the Atlantic.

Already American firms control 90 per cent of the West German computer industry and 90 per cent of the French. The British typewriter business is now nearly 100 per cent in American hands. In the crucial international balance of patent-payments, America has a five-to-one margin over Europe.

At the top of the world league are the countries of mass-technology, mass-production and mass-marketing. There are only two of them: the USA and Russia. Backed by the mass-effect of two hundred million hard-working people, they have achieved the real breakthrough. They are challenged today only by Japan. Europe has the potential but is not exploiting it.

In the balance today is the technological, industrial and cultural future of nations—in that sequence. Belatedly we have come to realize in the second half of the twentieth century that technology has become the mainspring and the preserver of ideology and culture. And success in the technological race is dependent on brains—and on brains *properly utilized*. The very scale of modern economic problems has accelerated the onset of the Knowledge Revolution. As problems increase in breadth and complexity, more and more brainpower is needed.

Europe is still the home of civilization, but she *must* protect

her future. There are no short-term solutions to the problems—
no easy, or inexpensive ways out. But unless Europe takes action
now her future generations are condemned to a third-rate twilight
existence—and the responsibility will lie with the present
generation.

The problem is to some extent a circular one. Europe urgently
needs the brains to solve her problems and to create the mass
technology that will make her competitive. But she needs the
technology to attract and keep the brains. Breaking out of this
circle is going to take vigorous enlightened thinking, courageous
decision-making, the sinking of national prides and prejudices, and
a lot of hard work.

ABOUT THE AUTHOR

Professor Dimitris Chorafas is uniquely qualified to take a world view of the Knowledge Revolution. His dual status as international management consultant and cosmopolitan University Professor has taken him to 43 different countries in four continents in the last ten years. He speaks English, French, Spanish and Greek fluently and is proficient in Russian and German.

Professor Chorafas' international business experience has been most extensive. In his early career he was engaged on mathematical simulators, systems engineering and executive development with I.B.M. in Europe and the U.S.A. He was Director, Management Information Systems, with the giant American consultant firm of Booz, Allen and Hamilton International Inc. Since then, as a corporate management consultant in his own practice based in Paris, he has worked with Bull-General Electric; Allegemeine Elektricitäts Gesellschaft (AEG) and Telefunken; Compagnie Française Thomson-Houston; Nestlé; UNIVAC in the U.K., Europe, and Scandinavia; Pechiney; Osram GmbH; Omega (Louis Brandt et Frère, S.A.); Olivetti; ANTAR—Pétroles de l'Atlantique; National Iranian Oil Company; Finnish Defence Forces; Compagnie Générale Transatlantique (French Line); American Management Association, and Management Centre/Europe. His projects have ranged from top-level company re-organisation to market strategy, operations research, electronic data processing and long-term corporate planning. He has conducted seminars on executive development for C.S.F.; Shell-France; Le Matériel Téléphonique; C.R.C.; the Polish Academy of Sciences, and the French Army.

A Fulbright scholar, he received his education at such diverse institutions as the Sorbonne (Docteur de l'Université de Paris en Mathématique), the University of California (M.S.E.), the University of Denver, and George Washington University. His first degree, in mechanical and electrical engineering, was from the National Technical University, Athens, Greece. He has been Professor of Engineering at the Catholic University of America, Visiting Professor of Information Science and Business Administration at Washington State University, Visiting Professor at the Centre of Industrial Studies of the University of Geneva, and since 1968, Visiting Professor, School of Information Science, Georgia Institute of Technology.

He has had over 30 major works published in eight countries.